ALBANIAN-ENGLISH
ENGLISH-ALBANIAN
DICTIONARY AND
PHRASEBOOK

ALBANIAN-ENGLISH ENGLISH-ALBANIAN DICTIONARY AND PHRASEBOOK

RAMAZAN JOHN HYSA

HIPPOCRENE BOOKS
New York

This book is dedicated to the long-suffering Albanian people of Kosova, to whom I wish a safe and peaceful life in their ancestral land.

CONTENTS

FOREWORD

The *Albanian-English/English-Albanian Dictionary and Phrasebook* contains about 2,000 English words and their equivalents in Albanian, as well as more than 1,500 useful phrases for everyday situations. This book was written to facilitate day-to-day communication between members of the peace-keeping mission, aid workers etc. in Albania, Kosovo, and Macedonia, and the Albanian people and the local representatives.

ABBREVIATIONS

f. feminine
fig. figurative
m. masculine
n. noun
pl. plural
poss. possessive
pron. pronoun
sb. somebody
sg. singular
sth. something
v. verb

PRONUNCIATION GUIDE

Albanian letter	Approximate (English) equivalent	Albanian example
Vowels		
a	father	**bar'** (grass)
e	set	**lejlek'** (stork)
ë	hurt	**hë'në** (moon)
i	see	**liri'** (freedom)
o	more	**o'rë** (hour)
u	put	**puth** (to kiss)
y	as in French une	**py'kë** (peg)
Consonants		
b	book	**bu'kë** (bread)
c	pizza	**ce'kët** (shallow)
ç	check	**çora'pe** (socks)
d	dear	**dru** (wood)
dh	this	**dhe** (earth)
f	free	**fus** (to put in)
g	go	**grup** (group)
gj	judge	**gji'thë** (all)
h	heart	**hap** (to open)
j	year	**josh** (to attract)
k	kiss	**kaloj'** (to pass)
l	left	**lu'aj** (to move)
ll	ball	**pa'llë** (sword)
m	make	**pe'më** (tree)
n	noon	**nis** (to begin)
nj	news	**njoh** (to know)
p	pray	**pres** (to wait)

q	cheese, but softer, as if combined with l	qu'aj (to call)
r	room	rendor' (ordinal)
rr	borrow	bu'rrë (man)
s	silk	su'pë (soup)
sh	sheep	shi'fër (cipher)
t	toy	tullac' (bald)
th	thief	thi'thë (nipple)
v	van	vaj'zë (girl)
x	ads	xunkth (rush)
xh	jaw	xhep (pocket)
z	zone	zor (difficulty)
zh	vision	zhur'më (noise)

As you can see, Albanian has nine letters consisting of consonant combinations:

dh, gj, ll, nj, rr, sh, th, xh and zh

They are pronounced simultaneously as one distinct sound. The closest pronunciation of these letters is given above.

Albanian has no silent letters. Every letter is pronounced, and it is always pronounced the same way. The only exception is the vowel ë, which is almost silent at the end of a word, for example **bu'kë** (bread) is pronounced *bu:'k* rather than *bu'kë*. Likewise, **tekni'kë** is pronounced *tekni:'k* rather than *tekni'kë*. Of course, this doesn't apply to words like **ve'tëm**, **tea'tër**, where ë is in the middle of the word.

In this book, the apostrophe (') is used to mark the stressed syllable, which is always the syllable preceding the apostrophe. For example, the word **lëviz'** (move) is pronounced *lëVIZ* (with the stress on VIZ).

A VERY BASIC GRAMMAR

Nouns

As a rule, nouns ending in a consonant are masculine. Most nouns ending in **-ë** are feminine. Also, most nouns ending in a stressed **-a** or **-e** are feminine. Neuter nouns are rare, and the reader doesn't have to bother about them. In general, the Albanian gerund is a neuter noun. It is always preceded by the particle **-të**, for example **të qa'rë - të qa'rët** (crying); **të e'cur - të e'curit** (walking).

Articles

In Albanian, as in English, the noun has two forms, indefinite and definite. The indefinite article **një** is the equivalent of the English 'a', for example **një gru'a** (a woman), **një bu'rrë** (a man), but in most situations you don't need to use it. For instance 'I am a man' is simply translated **U'në jam bu'rrë**.

The definite article is added to the noun. Masculine nouns add **-i** in their definite form:
    bu'rr/ë (man) - **bu'rri** (the man).
    komb (nation) - **ko'mbi** (the nation)
    bilbi'li (nightingale) - **bilbili** (the nightingale)

Nouns ending in **-g**, **-h**, or **-k** add the ending **-u**:
    shteg (footpath)- **shte'gu** (the footpath)
    bark (belly) - **bar'ku** (the belly).

Feminine nouns change their ending to **-a** in their definite form:

> **bu'kë** (bread) - **bu'ka** (the bread)
> **shkretëti'rë** (desert) - **shkretëti'ra** (the desert)

Feminine nouns ending in a stressed **-a** or **-e** add the ending **-ja** in their definite form:

> **suva'** (plaster)- **suva'ja** (the plaster)
> **fole'** (nest) - **fole'ja** (the nest)
> **gru'a** (woman)- **gru'aja** (the woman)

When the **-e** is not stressed, it is dropped before adding **-ja**:

> **qo'she** (corner) - **qo'shja** (the corner).

Plural

Generally speaking, most masculine nouns add **-e** or **-ë** in the plural, and an additional **-t** in the definite plural:

> **mal** (mountain) - **ma'le** (mountains) - **ma'let**
>   (the mountains)
> **flamur'** (flag) - **flamu'rë** (flags) - **flamu'rët**
>   (the flags)

Most feminine nouns ending in a stressed **-a** or **-e** have a plural identical with the singular; they add **-të** in the definite plural:

> **para'** (money) - **para'** (moneys) - **para'të** (the
>   moneys)
> **fole'** (nest) - **fole'** (nests) - **fole'të** (the nests).

Declension

Albanian nouns are declined. Here are some declined masculine and feminine nous:

fat (luck) m.

	Indefinite singular	Definite singular
Nominative	një fat	fa'ti
Genitive	i/e një fa'ti	i/e fa'tit
Dative	një fa'ti	fa'tit
Accusative	një fat	fa'tin

	Indefinite plural	Definite plural
Nominative	fa'te	fa'tet
Genitive	i/e fa'teve	i/e fa'teve
Dative	fa'teve	fa'teve
Accusative	fa'te	fa'tet

kapak (cover) m.

	Indefinite singular	Definite singular
Nominative	një kapak'	kapa'ku
Genitive	i/e një kapa'ku	i/e kapa'kut
Dative	një kapa'ku	kapa'kut
Accusative	një kapak'	kapa'kun

	Indefinite plural	Definite plural
Nominative	kapa'kë	kapa'kët
Genitive	i/e kapa'këve	i/e kapa'këve
Dative	kapa'këve	kapa'këve
Accusative	kapa'kë	kapa'kët

ku'pë (cup) f.

	Indefinite singular	Definite singular
Nominative	një ku'pë	ku'pa
Genitive	i/e një ku'pe	i/e ku'pës
Dative	një ku'pe	ku'pës
Accusative	një ku'pë	ku'pën

	Indefinite plural	*Definite plural*
Nominative	ku'pa	ku'pat
Genitive	i/e ku'pave	i/e ku'pave
Dative	ku'pave	ku'pave
Accusative	ku'pa	ku'pat

lu'le (flower) f.

	Indefinite singular	*Definite singular*
Nominative	një lu'le	lul'ja
Genitive	i/e një lu'leje	i/e lu'les
Dative	një lu'leje	lu'les
Accusative	një lu'le	lu'len

	Indefinite plural	*Definite plural*
Nominative	lu'le	lu'let
Genitive	i/e lu'leve	i/e lu'leve
Dative	lu'leve	lu'leve
Accusative	lu'le	lu'let

Adjectives

In Albanian, the adjective usually follows the noun:
>   **di'të e bu'kur** (nice day)
>   **bu'rrë trim** (brave man)

Descriptive adjectives or qualifiers are mostly articulated adjectives, i.e. adjectives preceded by the particle **i** for masculine, **e** for feminine and **të** for plural adjectives.
>   **i mi'rë** (good) m. - **e mi'rë** f.- **të mi'rë** m. pl. -
>   **të mi'ra** f. pl.

However, there are also unarticulated adjectives, i.e. adjectives that are combined with a noun without any preceding particle:

bu'rrë besnik (faithful man) - **gru'a besni'ke** (faithful woman) - **bu'rra besni'kë** (faithful men) - **gra besni'ke** (faithful women)

When declined, the articulated adjectives change the masculine article **i** or the feminine article **e** to **të** or **e**, for example:

kapak (cover) m. **+ i bukur** (beautiful)

	Indefinite plural	*Definite plural*
Nominative	një kapak' i bu'kur	kapa'kët e bu'kur
Genitive	i/e një kapa'ku të bu'kur	i/e kapa'këve të bu'kur
Dative	një kapa'ku të bu'kur	kapa'këve të bukur
Accusative	një kapak' i bu'kur	kapa'kët e bu'kur

vaj'zë (girl) **+ e pa'shme** (beautiful)

	Indefinite singular	*Definite plural*
Nominative	një vaj'zë e pa'shme	vaj'zat e pa'shme
Genitive	i/e një vaj'ze të pa'shme	i/e vaj'zave të pa'shme
Dative	një vaj'ze të pa'shme	vaj'zave të pa'shme
Accusative	një vaj'zë të pa'shme	vaj'zat e pa'shme

Possessive adjectives

Possessive adjectives in general are placed after the noun:

Masculine singular	*Masculine plural*
li'bri im (my book)	**li'brat e mi** (my books)
li'bri yt (your book)	**li'brat e tu** (your books)
li'bri i tij/i saj	**li'brat e tij/e saj**
(his/her book)	(his/her books)
li/bri jo'në (our book)	**li'brat ta'në** (our books)
li'bri ju'aj (your book)	**li'brat tu'aj** (your books)
li'bri i ty're	**li'brat e ty're**
(their book)	(their books)

Feminine singular	*Feminine plural*
to'ka i'me (my land)	**to'kat e mi'a** (my lands)
to'ka jo'te (your land)	**to'kat e tu'a** (your lands)
to'ka e tij/e saj	**to'kat e tij/e saj**
(his/her land)	(his/her lands)
to'ka jo'në (our land)	**to'kat to'na** (our lands)
to'ka ju'aj (your land)	**to'kat tu'aja** (your lands)
to'ka e ty're	**to'kat e ty're**
(their land)	(their lands)

Personal Pronouns

Nominative	
u'në	I
ti	you
ai'/ajo'	he/she
ne	we
ju	you
ata'/ato'	they

Dative

mu'a	me
ty	you
atij'/asaj'	him/her
ne've	us
ju've	you
aty're	them

Accusative

mu'a	me
ty	you
atë'	him/her
ne	us
ju	you
ata'/ato'	them

Demonstrative Pronouns

Nominative

ky/kjo	this
ai/ajo	that
këta'/këto'	these
ata'/ato'	those

Genitive

i/e këtij'/kësaj'	of this
atij'/asaj'	of that
i/e këty're	of these
i/e aty're	of those

Dative

këtij'/kësaj	to this
atij'/asaj'	to that
këty're	to these
aty're	to those

Accusative
këtë'   this
atë'   that
këta'/këto'   these
ata'/ato'   those

The Verb

The verb in Albanian has nine moods: indicative, subjunctive, conditional, imperative, infinitive, participle, gerund, admirative and optative. The indicative has no less than eight tenses. Here is a regular verb in the first person singular in all the eight tenses of the indicative:

(u'në) jetoj' = (I) live

Present	*Imperfect*	*Simple past*
jetoj'	**jeto'ja**	**jeto'va**
(I live)	(I used to live)	(I lived)

Present perfect	*Past perfect*	*Pluperfect*
kam jetu'ar	**ki'sha jetu'ar**	**pa'ta jetu'ar**
(I have lived)	(I had lived)	(I had lived)

Future	*Future perfect*
do të jetoj'	**do të kem jetu'ar**
(I will live)	(I will have lived)

And, just for fun, have a look at the admirative and optative moods, which do not exist in English. Both of them have two tenses:

Admirative

Present	*Past*
jeto'kam	**pa'skam jetu'ar**
(how strange it is that I am living!)	(how strange it is that I have been living!)

Optative mood

Present	*Past*
jeto'fsha	**pa'ça jetu'ar**
(I wish I lived)	(I wish I had lived)

Word Order

The Albanian word order is usually as follows:
  noun + adjective + verb + object + adverb,
    complement, etc., for example:
  Një mësu'es i ri fillo'i pu'në dje në shko'llën to'në.
  (A new teacher started work yesterday in our school.)

ALBANIAN - ENGLISH
SHQIP - ANGLISHT

A

aeroplan' airplane
aeroport' airport
a'fër near; close by
afërsisht nearly
afi'she poster
aftësi' ability
agim' dawn; daybreak
ai he
a'jër air
aj'kë cream
aj'kë e thar'të sour cream
ajo' she
ajro're, po'stë airmail
ako'ma yet
aksident' accident
a'kull ice
akullo're ice cream
a'lo (në telefon') hello! (on the phone)
ambulan'cë ambulance
a'në side
ani'je ship
anke'së complaint
anullim' cancellation
aparat' (fotografik') camera
apartament' apartment
apendisit' appendicitis
ar gold
ardh'me, e future

ar'dhur, të arrivals
argëtim' pastime
argjend' silver
ari' bear n.
ar'më zja'rri firearm
armëpushim' cease-fire; truce
armik' enemy
arsy'e reason
artist' artist
arrij' arrive; come
asgjë' nothing
asgjëku'ndi nowhere
askund' nowhere
askush' nobody
asnjëhe'rë never
asnjë'ri none; neither
aspak' not at all; not in the least; by no means
a'shpër, i/e tough
ashtu' so; like that
ata' they; those
atje' there
ato' they; those
autostop' hitchhiking
avokat' lawyer

B

baba'/ba'bë father; dad
bagazh' luggage
bakshish' tip n.
bal'të mud
ballkon' balcony
bamirësi' charity
bar grass; hay
bar bar; pub; saloon

bar (mjekësor') medication
bar'dhë, i white
bari'shte herbs
bark belly; stomach; diarrhea
bar'ku, he'qje diarrhea
ba'një bathroom
ba'rrë, me pregnant
ba'shkë; së ba'shku together
bashkëshort' husband
bela' trouble
benzi'në gasoline
beqar' single; not married
berber' hairdresser
besoj' believe
bezdis' annoy
bezdis'shëm, i/e (-shme) annoying
bëj make; do
bëj dashuri' make love
bëj lu'ftë wage war
bë'hem become
bibliote'kë library
bi'e fall down
bi'jë/vaj'zë daughter
bilar'do pool; billiards
biletari' ticket office
bile'të ticket
bile'të vaj'tje-ar'dhje return ticket
bile'të ve'tëm vaj'tje one-way ticket
binja'kë twins
bir son
bise'dë conversation
bisko'ta të kri'pura crackers
bi'shë beast
bize'le peas
biznes' business
blej buy v.

ble'të bee
blu dark blue
bllokim' qarkulli'mi/trafi'ku traffic jam
bojëka'fe brown
bojëqi'elli light blue
bo'jë color
bo'rë snow
borxh debt
borxh, marr borrow
bo'të world
bra'vë lock n.
bredh, e (një vend) explore (an area)
breg (de'ti, liqe'ni) shore
bre'kë panties
bre'nda inside
bre'nda në into
bretko'së frog
bru'më dough
budalla' stupid; fool
bujk farmer
bujqësi' agriculture
bu'kë bread
bu'kur, i/e pretty; beautiful; lovely
bukuri' beauty
burg prison
burim' spring; water source
bu'rrë man; husband
buzëqesh' smile v.
buzëqe'shje smile n.

C

certifika'të li'ndjeje birth certificate
ciga're, pi smoke a cigarette

cilë'si quality
ci'li who; which
co'pa a piece

Ç

ça'dër umbrella; tent
çaj tea
çan'të shpi'ne backpack
çast moment
çdo any; every
çdo njeri' everyone
çe'lës key
çe'lët, i/e light (color)
çerek' quarter
çë'shtje issue; question
çfa'rë what
çfarëdo' any
çfarëdoqo'ftë anything
çifut' Jewish
çim'kë bug
çiz'me boots
çlirim' liberation
çlo'dhem relax
çlo'dhës relaxing
çme'ndur, i/e mad; crazy
çmim price
çmim (i fitu'ar) prize (won)
çmu'ar, i/e precious
ço'hem get up
ço'hu! get up!; get out of bed!
çora'pe socks
çudit'shëm, i/e (-shme) strange; funny

D

dal go out
da'lje exit
da'lje siguri'mi emergency exit
dar'dhë pear
dar'kë dinner; supper
das'më wedding
da'shur, i nice; kind
da'shur, i/e boyfriend; girlfriend; partner;
    sweetheart
dashuroj' love v.
de'le sheep
dembel' lazy
dentist' dentist
de'ri until
derr pig
det sea
detyrim' obligation
dëbo'rë snow
dëgjoj' listen; hear
dëmtim' injury
dër'goj send
dëshiroj' wish v.
dëshmi' aftësi'e driver's licence
dëshpërim' broken heart
di know
diçka' something
di'ell sun
di'ell, me sunny
dikur' once; long ago
dikush' someone
dil'ni! get out!
di'mër winter
disa' some; several; a few
disi' somehow

di'të day
ditëli'ndje birthday
dja'lë boy; youth; son
djall; dreq devil
dja'thë cheese
dja'thë i bar'dhë feta cheese
djath'tas right; to the right
djath'të, i/e right
dje yesterday
do'bët, i/e weak
dobi'shëm, i/e (-shme) useful; helpful
doga'në customs (at borders)
doma'te tomato
domosdo'shëm, i/e (-shme) indispensable; vital
do'rë hand
do'sje file; record
dre deer
drejt; në drejtim' të towards
drej'ta të njeri'ut, të human rights
drej'të, i/e just; fair
drejtësi' justice; fairness
drejtim' direction; course; route
drejtues administrator
dre'kë lunch
dreq devil
drita're window
dri'të trafi'ku traffic light
dru wood
dru zja'rri firewood
dry padlock; lock
du'a want; wish; love v.
du'a të... I want to...
duhan' tobacco
duhanpi'rës smoker
du'het need; must v.
du'ket look; appear

dyqan' i madh department store
dyshek' mattress

Dh

dhe ground; earth
dhe and
dhëmb tooth
dhë'mballë molar
dhi goat
dhi'mbje pain; **dhi'mbje dhë'mbi** toothache;
    dhi'mbje ko'ke headache
dhi'mbje me'si backache
dho'më room
dhu'në violence
dhura'të present; gift; donation

E

e'ci walk v.
e'cje hike n.
e'dhe and
e'dhe një' extra; one more
e'dhe sikur' even if
e'gër, i/e (kafshë) wild (not tame)
ej! there!
ekspozi'të exhibition
e'mër name n.
emigrant' emigrant
e'nde yet
energji' energy
epidemi' epidemic
e'rë wind
e'rrët, i/e dark

e'tje thirst
e'tje, kam be thirsty
etur, i/e thirsty
e'the fever

Ë

ë'mbël, i/e sweet
ëmbëlsi' sweetness
ëmbëlsi'rë cookie; biscuit; dessert
ë'ndërr dream n.

F

fabri'kë factory
fakultet' faculty; college
fal, më; fal'ni, më I apologize
fa'las free (of charge)
falemnde'rit thank you
fami'lje family
fa'rë seed
farmaci' pharmacy
fasu'le beans
fat, me lucky
fatkeq' unhappy
fatkeqësi' accident
fatkeqësisht' unfortunately
fatu'rë check; bill n.
fe'mër female adj., n.
femëror', -'re feminine
fermer' farmer
ferr hell
fe'stë holiday; fe'stë zyrta're public holiday
fëmi'jë child

fik (ra'dion) switch off
fi'két, mё bi'e tё pass out
fillim' beginning; start
filloj' begin
fir'mё signature
firmos' sign v.
fitoj win
fja'la, me qё ra by the way
fjalor' dictionary
flak throw (away)
flamur' flag
flas talk; speak
fle sleep v.
flo'kё hair
floktar' hairdresser
flori' gold
flu'tur butterfly
fluturim' flight
fol mё ngada'lё slow down
fo'lёs speaker
for'tё, i/e strong
fotografi' picture; photo
fotografoj' take a picture
fqinj neighbor
fre'skёt, i/e cool; fresh
fri'kё fear n.
fri'kё, kam be afraid (of)
fri'kё, mos ki' don't be afraid
frut fruit
fshat village; countryside
fshatar' peasant; farmer
fsheh'tё, i/e secret
fte'sё invitation
fto'hem catch a cold
ftoh'tё, i/e cold
ftoh'tё, marr tё catch a cold

ftoj invite
ftu'ar, i/e guest
fund bottom; end
fundit, i/e last; final
fuqi' power; might
fuqi'shëm, i/e (-shme) powerful
fur'çë brush n.
fur'çë dhë'mbësh toothbrush
fu'rrë bu'ke bakery
fustan' dress n.
fy'ej insult v.
fy'erje insult n.
fyty'rë face n.

G

gabim' mistake; fault
gabu'ar, i/e wrong
gafo'rre crab
galeri' ar'ti art gallery
ga'rë race; competition
ga'ti ready
gat'shëm, i/e (-shme) ready; prepared
gatu'aj cook v.
gaz gas
gaz natyror' natural gas
gazetar' journalist
gaze'të newspaper
gënje'shtër lie n.
gështe'një chestnut
gëzu'ar' i/e glad
gi'dë turisti'ke guidebook
godi'në bani'mi apartment block
gomar' donkey
gra women

grabi'tje robbery
gri'ndje fight n.
grip flu
gro'pë hole
gro'shë beans
gru'a woman; wife
gru'rë wheat
gur rock; stone

Gj

gjak blood
gjal'pë butter
gja'llë, i/e living; lively; vivid
gjallëri' liveliness
gjar'për snake
gja'të, i/e long; tall
gjej find
gjel'bër, i/e green
gjelde'ti turkey
gje'llë meal; dish
gje'llë e ngroh'të hot food
gje'ndje civi'le marital status
gje'pura nonsense
gje'rë, i/e wide
gjë thing
gjëmon' thunder v.
gjë'ra me vle'rë valuables
gjithashtu' also
gjithçka' all; everything
gji'thë, i/e all; complete; the whole thing
gjithmo'në/gjithnjë' always
gji'zë cottage cheese
gju knee
gju'hë language

gjyka'tës/gjyqtar' judge
gjymty'rë artificia'le artificial limb
gjynah'! it's a pity!
gjy'smë half n.
gjysh grandfather
gjy'she grandmother

H

ha eat
habi' surprise; shock
habit'shëm, i/e (-shme) amazing
hap open
ha'pje pill
ha'pur, i/e open adj.
hardhi' vine
harroj' forget
hedh throw (away)
he'kur iron n.
hekuros' iron v.
hekuru'dhë railway
he'rë pas he're now and then
he'rët early
hë'në e plo'të full moon
hiç nil
hi'dhem jump v.
hi'dhur, i/e bitter
hi'je shadow
hij'shëm, i/e (-shme) charming
ho'lla, të cash; change n.
ho'llë, i/e thin; slim
hua', jap lend
hua', marr borrow
huadhë'nës lender; loan-giver
hu'aj lend; borrow

hu'aj, i stranger; foreigner
hu'aj, i/e foreign
humb lose
humbas' ndje'njat pass out
humor' humor; sense of humor
hu'ndë nose
hyr'je entrance

I

ibrik' kettle
i'ki go away
ilaç' medication
i'mi; i'mja mine poss. pron.
imigrant' immigrant
imigrim' immigration
infeksion' infection
infermie're nurse
insekt' bug
interesant' interesting
interurba'ne, telefona'të long-distance call
i'shull island

J

jam be
jap give
ja'shtë outdoors
jashtëzakon'shëm, i/e (-shme) unusual
ja'vë week
jeshil', -e green
je'të life
jetim' orphan
jo no

jo'miqësor' unfriendly
jo'në our
ju'aj your
jug south

K

ka'fe coffee
kafsha'të bite n.
ka'fshë animal
kafshoj' bite v.
kalem' pencil
ka'lë horse
kalkulatri'çe calculator
kaloj' pra'në pass by
kal'tër, i/e blue; light blue
kalu'ar, e past n.
kalu'ar, i/e last; past adj.
kam have
kam borxh' owe
kamion' truck
kamp camp; camping
kamp refugja'tësh refugee camp
karburant' fuel
kartoli'në postcard
kastravec' cucumber
karri'ge chair
karro'cë me ka'lë horse and cart
ka'u, mish beef
kek cake
keq, i/e (-'qe) bad; nasty
keq, më worse
keq, më vjen sorry; I'm sorry
keqar'dhje sympathy
ke'qe, me e'rë të smelly

keqkuptim' misunderstanding
këmbej' para' exchange money
këmbësor' pedestrian
këmbim' parash' change; money exchange
këmi'shë shirt
këndoj' sing
kënd'shëm, i/e (-shme) lovely; pleasant; enjoyable
kë'ngë song
këpu'cë shoes
këpur'dha mushrooms
kërcej' dance; jump v.
kërcim' dancing
kërkoj' ask for; require; look for
kështje'llë castle
kështu' so; like this
këta' these
këto' these
këtu' here
ki me'ndjen! take care!
kikiri'kë peanuts
kinema' cinema; movies
kirurg' surgeon
ki'shë church
kjo this
koc'kë bone
koçek' barn
ko'dër hill
ko'hë time; duration; weather
ko'hë e li'rë spare/free time
ko'kë head n.
komb nation
kombësi' nationality
kombëtar' national
komshi' neighbor
kontrabandist' smuggler
koprac' stingy

kopsht garden
ko'rra, të harvest; crops
ko'rrje harvesting
korrupsion' corruption
kos yogurt
ko'vë bucket; pail
krah arm
krejt quite
krenar' proud
krenari' pride
krevat' bed
krim crime
kri'me lu'fte war crimes
kri'pë salt
kri'pur, i/e salty
kri'zë ze'mre heart attack
kru'arje itch
kryeqytet' capital city
kryesor' main
kryqëzim' intersection; crossroads
Kry'qi i Kuq Red Cross/Crescent
kthe'hem turn around
kthe'hu maj'tas/djath'tas! turn left/right!
kthe'së e plo'të U-turn
kthim return n.
ku where
kudo' everywhere
kudoqo'ftë anywhere
kufi' border
kujdes' care n.
kujdes'! take care!; look out!
kujde'sem take care of
kujdes'shëm, i/e (-shme) careful
kujtoj' remember
kule'të wallet; purse
ku'llë tower

ku'ndërt, i/e reverse; opposite n.
kuptoj' understand
kuq', i red
kur when
kur've prostitute
ku'rrë never
kurrgjë' nothing
kurriz' back n. (body)
kurrkund' nowhere
kusur' rest; change n.
kush who
kushdo' anyone; everyone
kushëri', -ri'rë cousin
kushtu'eshëm, i/e (-eshme) expensive
kuti' posta're mailbox
kuzhi'në kitchen
kuzhinier' cook n.
ky this
ky'çur, i/e locked

L

la'gur, i/e wet
la'hem wash; bathe
laj wash v.
laj'me news
lakuriq' naked
laps pencil
larg far
larg', më farther
largësi' shiki'mi visibility
lar'gët, i far; remote
largo'hem go away
lart up
lar'të, i/e high; loud (voice)

lartësi' height
la'shtë, i/e ancient
leh'të, i/e easy; light
lejoj' allow
le'pur rabbit
lesh wool
le'tër letter
letërnjofti'mi identification
lexoj' read v.
lëku'rë skin; leather
lëndim' injury
lëng fru'tash fruit juice
lëviz' move v.
li'bër book n.
li'bër bisedi'mesh phrasebook
librari' bookstore
ligj law
lind be born; give birth
lind (di'elli) rise (sun)
li'ndje birth
li'ndje east
li'ndje e di'ellit sunrise
li'ndur, i/e born
liqen' lake
li'rë, i/e free adj.
li'rë, i/e cheap
liri' freedom
li'stë gje'llësh; meny' menu
lo'dhur, i/e tired
lo'jë game
lokal' bar; pub; saloon
lo'pe, mish beef
lo'pë cow
lu'aj play v.
lu'ftë war
lu'gë spoon

lugi'në valley
lu'le flower
lu'më river
lum'tur, i/e happy
lu'tem, të please

Ll

llastu'ar, i/e spoiled fig.
llogari' check; bill n.
llogaritar' accountant
lloj kind; sort; variety
lloj-lloj various; all kinds of

M

ma'ce cat
madh, i/e (-e) large
mahnit'shëm, i/e (-shme) amazing
maj'të, i/e left (side)
makaro'na pasta; macaroni
mal mountain
ma'lli, më merr (për dikë') miss sb.
mallu'ar, i homesick
ma'po department store
marte'së marriage; wedding
martu'ar, i/e married
marr take; get
marr në telefon' call v.
ma'rrë, i/e mad; crazy
marrëve'shje agreement
ma'së (këpu'ce etj) size (of shoes etc,)
ma'shkull male n.
mata'në accross; beyond

mba'rë!, të shko'ftë good luck!
mbaroj' finish v.
mbaru'a, u... we ran out of...
mba'thje panties
mbe'së niece; granddaughter
mbërrij' arrive; come
mbi on; over
mbie'mër last name
mbipe'shë overweight
mbrapsht backwards; in reverse
mbrë'mje evening
mbrë'mje argëti'mi evening party
mbroj protect
mbroj'tje protection
mbyll shut; close; lock; switch off
mby'llur, i/e closed; locked; off
me with
megji'thëse although
mençuri' wisdom
mend, sjell ndër remember
mendim' thought
me'ndje mind
me'ndje, ndërroj' change one's mind
mendoj' think
menjëhe'rë immediately
merako'sur, i/e worried
mes middle
mesatar' average; medium-sized
mesdi'të middday
mesna'të midnight
më mi'rë rather; I'd rather
më në fund! at last!
mëha'llë neighborhood
mëlçi' liver
mëngjes' morning; breakfast
mënja'në aside; apart

mërzi' boredom
mërzit'shëm, i/e (-shme) boring; annoying
mësim', jap teach
mësoj' learn; teach
mësu'es teacher
mi rat; mouse
mi'ell flour
mik friend; guest
mikpri'tje hospitality
milingo'në ant
minie'rë qymy'ri coal mine
mi'rë, i/e good; kind; nice
mi'rë, më better
mirësevjen'! welcome!
mi'ri, më i; -mi'ra, më e best
mirupa'fshim good-bye
mi'sër corn
mish meat
mish de'rri pork
mish vi'çi veal
mi'zë fly n.
mi'zë dhe'u ant
mjaft enough; quite
mjal'të honey
mje'gull fog
mje'kërr beard
mje'shtër master
mo'de, i da'lë old-fashioned
mo'llë apple
mo'shë age
mot next year
mot weather
mot me e'rë windy weather
mo'tër sister
mpreh'të, i/e sharp
mu'aj month

mulli' mill
mund can; may
mund beat v.
mu'ndet maybe
mundësi' possibility
mundësi', ka probably
mundshëm, i/e (-shme) possible
mu'shkë mule
mushkëri' lung
mushko'një mosquito
mysafir' guest

N

na'ftë oil
na'të night
naty'rë countryside
natyr'shëm, i/e (-shme) natural
ndaj take apart
nda'lem; ndaloj' stop v.
ndalim' stop n.
ndaloj' forbid; stop
nda'rë, i/e divorced; separated
nder'shëm, i/e (-shme) honest
ndershmërisht'? honestly?
ndez turn on; switch on
ndërma'rrje business enterprise
ndërte'së building
ndërtoj' build
ndërroj' shtëpi' move; change one's residence
ndërroj' vend change place
ndi'ej feel
ndih'më help; aid n.
ndih'më! help!
ndihmoj' help; aid v.

ndo'shta maybe
ndo'tur, i/e polluted
ndreq repair; fix
ndrit'shëm, i/e (-shme) light; shining
ndry'shëm, i/e (-shme) different
ndryshim' change; transformation
ne we
negociu'es negotiator
ne'sër tomorrow
ne've us
neveri'tur, i/e fed up with
nevo'jë për, kam need v.
nevoji'tet need v.
nevoj'shëm, i/e (-shme) necessary
në at; in
në shtëpi' at home
nën/ndën under
në'në mother
nënshkrim' signature
nënshkru'aj sign
në'për about; through; via
nëpërmjet' through; by; via
nëpu'nës employee; official
nëpu'nës i lar'të senior official
nëpu'nës shte'ti civil servant
nëse'; në qo'ftë se' if
nga from
ngada'lë slowly
ngadal'të, i/e slow
ngas maki'në drive a car
ngri'cë frost
ngri'hem get up
ngri'hu! get up!
ngroh heat v.
ngro'hës heater

ngroh'je heating
ngroh'të, i/e warm
ngu'shtë, i/e narrow adj.
ngja'rë, ka të probably
ngja'shëm, i/e (-shme) similar; like; alike
ngjy'rë color
nip nephew; grandson
ni'sje departure
nof'kë nickname
notoj' swim v.
nu'mër number
nxeh (dikë') annoy (sb.)
nxeh'të, i/e hot
nxehtësi' heat n.
nxe'hur, i/e mad; angry
nxë'nës student
nxitim' hurry n.
nxito'! hurry up!
ny'je (e kë'mbës) ankle

Nj

nje'rëz people
njerëzi'shëm, i/e (shme) human
njerëzor human
njeri' man
një kalim', rru'gë me one-way street
njëhe'rë; një he'rë once
njëj'të, i/e same
njëqind' one hundred
një'ri-tje'tri each other
njoftim' message

O

oqean' ocean
o'rë hour; clock; watch
o'rë do're wristwatch
o'rë e ha'pjes opening time
oriz' rice
ortak' business partner
ortek' avalanche
o'se or

P

pa without
paaftësi' disability
padrej'të, i/e unfair
paduru'eshëm, i/e (-shme) obnoxious
pagu'aj pay v.
pak a little bit
pak, më less
pake'të packet
paki'cë minority
pa'ko package
pak'tën, të at least
paligj'shëm, i/e (-shme) against the law
pallat' palace; apartment block
pa'mje view
pamu'ndur, i/e impossible
panxhar' beet
papërshtat'shëm, i/e (-shme) inconvenient
papje'kur, i/e raw; unripe
papu'në, i/e unemployed
pa'ra; përpa'ra before
para' money
para' në do'rë cash

paraj'së heaven
parakaloj' overtake
parapëlqim' preference
paraqes' introduce
parehat'shëm, i/e (-shme) uncomfortable
pa'rë, i/e first
pa'rë, më ago
park zoologjik' zoo
parti' party (political)
pas after; behind
pasak'të, i/e wrong
pasapor'të passport
pasdi'te afternoon
pasjell'shëm, i/e (-shme) rude
pa'stër, i/e neat; clean
pastroj' clean v.
pasu'es next
pa'sur, i/e rich
pa'shëm, i/e (-shme) handsome
pashëndet'shëm, i/e (-shme) unhealthy
pata'te potato
pata'te të sku'qura French fries
paten'të maki'ne driver's licence
pa'të goose
paturp', i shameful
pavarësi' independence
pava'rur, i/e independent
pe'më tree
pemi'shte orchard
peng pawn; hostage
perëndim' west
perëndim' i di'ellit sunset
periferi' suburb
peri'me vegetables
per'lë pearl
person' person

pe'shë weight
peshk fish n.
peshkim' fishing
pëlcet' blow up; explode
pëlqen', më like v.
përba'llë opposite; across from
përdor' use v.
përdhunim' rape n.
përdhunoj' rape v.
përfshi'rë, i/e included
përfundimtar' final
përfundoj' finish v.
përgji'gje answer n.
përgji'gjem answer v.
përgju'mësh sleepy
përja'shta outdoors
përkry'er, i/e perfect
përkthej' interpret; translate
përkthy'es interpreter; translator
përmby'tje flood
përmirësim' improvement
përndry'she otherwise
përpa'ra in front (of)
përparësi' priority
përru'a stream; torrent
përse' why
përshtat'shëm, i/e (-shme) convenient
përtac' lazy
përtej' across; over
përveç' except
përvo'jë, me experienced
përzi'erje mixture
pi drink v.
pickim' insect bite
pickon' (insek'ti) bite v. (insect)
pi'je drink n.

pikant' spicy
pikërisht! exactly!
pilaf ' pilaf; risotto
piper' pepper (black/white)
pi'rë, i/e drunk
pirun' fork
pi'stë, i/e dirty
pi'shëm, u'jë i drinking water
pishi'në swimming pool
pje'për watermelon
pje'shkë peach
plazh beach
pleh'ra rubbish; junk
plot crowded
plo'të, i/e total; whole; full
plotësisht quite; entirely
po yes
po qe se if
pohim' confession
po'pull people; nation
popullo're, valle/muzi'kë folk dancing/music
porosis' order (in a restaurant) v.
portokall' orange
posa'çëm, i/e (-me) special
postbllok' road block
po'stë ajro're airmail
po'shtë down; below
pra'në next to
pranve'rë spring (season)
pra'pa behind
preferoj' prefer
preferu'ar, i/e favorite
prej from; by
premtim' promise n.
premtoj' promise v.
presion' pressure

prezantoj' introduce
pri'ndër parents
pri'shet break down v.
pri'shur, i/e out of order; spoiled
prit! wait!
problem' problem; trouble
pronar' owner
provoj' try v.
pse why
publik' public
pu'lë chicken
pu'llë (po'ste) stamp
pu'në work; job
punoj' work v.
punon', nuk out of order
pus well; pit
pushim' break; cease n.
pushi'me vacation
pu'shkë rifle
puth kiss v.
pu'thje; pu'thur, e kiss n.
py'es ask
py'etje question
py'etje, bëj një ask a question
pyll woods; forest

Q

qa'fë neck
qa'fë ma'li pass (mountain)
qaj cry v.
qarkullim' traffic
qar'të, i/e obvious
qen dog
qe'ndër center; headquarters

qerami'kë pottery
qesh laugh v.
qe'shur, për të funny
qetësi' quiet; silence; peace
qetëso'hem rest; take it easy
qeveri' government
që nga since
qëndrue'shëm, i/e (-shme) enduring
qi'ell sky
qind hundred
qingj lamb
qira' rent
qira', marr me rent v.
qiri' candle
qo'she corner
qu'mësht milk
qytet' town; city
qytetar' citizen
qyte'ti i vje'tër old town

R

ra'cë race; ethnicity
racion' ushqi'mi food supply
ra'dhë queue; line
rast opportunity
ra'ste, me occasionally
ra'stit, i/e by chance; accidental; casual
rece'të prescription
reçel' jam n.
refugjat' refugee
rehat'shëm, i/e (-shme) comfortable
rekomandoj' recommend
rezer'vë back up
rë'ndë, i/e heavy

rëndësi'shëm, i/e (-shme) important
rë'rë sand
ri, i; re, e new; young
ro'së duck

Rr

rra'fshët, i/e flat; plain
rrafshi'në plain; flat land
rrah beat
rra'llë rarely; seldom
rra'llë, i/e rare; hard to find
rre'gull, në OK
rregulloj' fix; repair
rre'më, i/e (-me) false
rre'në lie n.
rre'pë turnip
rreth circle; district
rrethi'na suburbs
rrezik' danger; risk
rrezikoj' risk v.
rrezik'shëm, i/e (-shme) dangerous; risky
rrëmbej' grab; kidnap
rrëmu'jë mess
rrëno'ja ruins
rri stay v.
rrjedh gjak, më bleed
rro'ba clothes
rro'ba të pala'ra laundry
rrobaqe'pës dressmaker
rro'gë wage; salary
rrufe' thunderbolt
rru'gë road; street
rru'gë e kalu'eshme passable road
rru'gë e pashtru'ar rough; rough road

rru'gë qo'rre/pa kry'e dead end
rrush grapes

S

sa keq' që... it's a shame/a pity...
sak'të, i/e right; correct; exact
sapun' soap
semafor' traffic light
send thing
ser'të, i/e tough
sëmu'ndje veneria'ne venereal disease
sëmu'rë, i ill; sick
si how
SI'DA AIDS
sidoqo'ftë anyhow
siguri' safety
sigurim' insurance
sigurisht' certainly
si'gurt, i/e safe; certain
simpati' liking; fancy
si'përm, i/e (-me) top
sjell'shëm, i/e (-shme) polite
s'ka gjë I don't mind
s'ka përse' don't mention it; you're welcome
sodi'tje sightseeing
son'te tonight
sot today
spec pepper
specialist' expert
spital' hospital
spiun' spy
s'prish pu'në I don't mind
stacion' station
stacion' tre'ni train station

sta'llë stable
stilograf' fountain pen
stilolaps' ball-point pen
stoli' jewelry
student' college student
stuhi' storm n.
sulm attack n.
sulmoj' attack v.
su'pë soup
suxhuk' sausage
sy eye; eyes
sy'ze di'elli sunglasses

Sh

shah chess
shaka' joke; kidding
shaka', bëj joke v.
she'mbull example
she'një ndali'mi stop sign
sheqer' sugar
shes sell
shesh lo'jërash playground
shesh stacio'ni platform
shëmtu'ar, i/e ugly
shëndet' health
shëndet'shëm, i/e (-shme) healthy
shëndo'shë, i/e fat
shërbim' service
shëtis' walk v.
shëti'tje walk; ride; drive n.
shëti'tje me ka'lë horseback riding
shfaq'je play; show
shi rain
shij'shëm, i/e (-shme) delicious; tasty

shikim' eyesight
shiko'! look there!
shikoj' look; see
shi'she bottle
shi'tet it is for sale
shi'tje sale
shi'tje, në/për for sale
shkatërru'ar, i/e ruined
shken'cë science
shkencëtar' scientist
shkëlqy'eshëm, i/e (-shme) excellent
shkëmb rock
shkëpus' take apart
shkëmbej' exchange v.
shkoj go
shko'llë school
shkre'pëse matches
shkrepti'më thunder
shkre'të, i/e poor; unfortunate
shkru'aj write
shkur'tër, i/e short
shofer' driver
shoh look; see
shok companion; friend; boyfriend
sho'qe friend; girlfriend
shoqëru'es companion
shpejt fast; quickly
shpejt! hurry up!
shpej'të, i/e quick, fast
shpejtësi' speed
shpej'ti, së soon
shpe'llë cave
shpesh often
shpërngu'lur, i displaced person
shpërthen' blow up; explode
shpëtoj' escape; rescue v.

shpi'në back n.
shpirt soul
shpor'të basket
shpreh'je phrase
shqetësu'ar, i/e worried
shtab headquarters
shtatgja'të tall
shtathe'dhur slim
shtatza'në pregnant
shteg path
shter'së barren
shte'tas citizen
shtetësi' citizenship
shtëpi' home; house
shtëpi'je homemade
shtrat bed
shtrenj'të, i/e expensive
shtrënga'të storm; thunderstorm
shtrëngu'ar, i/e tight
shtri'het lies v.
shtyj push
shumi'cë majority
shurdh deaf
shu'më very; many; much; a lot
shu'më, më more

T

tabe'lë rrugo're road sign
takim' meeting
takoj' meet
tani' now
tashmë' already
ta'vëll duha'ni ashtray

tavoli'në table
tea'tër theater
telash' trouble; problem
te'për too much; too many
te'për vo'në too late
te'përmi, së too much
tërbim' rabies
tërësor' total
tërheq' pull
tërmet' earthquake
tifoz' spor'ti sports fan
tij, i/e his; her; its
tje'tër other; another
tmerr'shëm, i/e (-shme) terrible
to'kë ground; earth
top ball (toy); cannon
tortu'rë torture n.
trafik' traffic
tra'ngull cucumber
tra'stë bag
tre e gjy'smë three and a half; (time) half past
    three; three-thirty (3:30)
treg market
treg i zi' black market
tregoj' tell; show
tregti' trade; business
tren train
trishtu'ar, i/e sad
trye'zë table
tungjatje'ta! hello!
turbulli'rë (në ko'kë) hangover
tur'më crowd
turp'shëm, i/e (-shme) shy; shameful
tym smoke n.
tymos' smoke cigarettes

Th

thartë, i/e sour
tha'të, i/e dry adj.
them say; tell
thërras' call v.
thi'kë knife
thje'shtë, i/e simple; easy; plain; not fancy
thy'ej break v.
thy'erje fracture
thy'eshëm, i/e (-shme) fragile
thy'het break v.

U

udhëhe'qës leader
udhërrëfy'es guide n.
udhëtar' passenger; traveller
udhëtim journey; trip
udhëtoj' travel v.
u'jë water n.
u'jë i pi'shëm drinking water
ujëva'rë waterfall
ujk wolf
u'lem sit down
u'lu! duck!
ulli' olive
u'në I
universitet' university; college
urdhëro'! here you are! (giving sth to sb.)
u'rë bridge
urgjent' urgent
uri'me! congratulations!
uri'tur, i/e hungry
urtësi' wisdom

urrej' hate v.
ushqim' food
ushtar' soldier
ushtri' çlirimta're liberation army
ushtroj' practice
usta' master; skilled person
u'thull vinegar

V

vaj'tje-ar'dhje, bile'të return ticket
vaj'zë girl
vaj'zë e re' young lady
vakt meal
vali'xhe suitcase
va'lle dance n.
va'lle populo're folk dancing
vallëzim' dancing
vallëzoj' dance v.
var'fër, i/e poor
var'kë boat
varr grave
varre'zë cemetery
varrim' funeral
vdes die v.
vde'kje death
vde'kur, i/e dead
ve, e widow
veç except
veçan'të, i/e special; particular
veçu'ar, i/e isolated; separate
veju'shë widow
ve'lur, i/e fed up with
vend place; country
vend të, në instead of

ventilator' fan
ver'bër, i/e blind; blind man
ver'dhë, i/e yellow
ve'rë wine
ve'rë summer
veri' north
vesh dress; put on; wear
vesh ear
ve'shje clothes
ve'shkë kidney
ve'të (unë, ti, ai, ajo, ne, ju, ata, ato) myself; yourself; himself; herself; itself; ourselves; yourselves; themselves
ve'tëm alone; only
vetëti'më lightning
vetmu'ar, i/e alone
ve'zë egg
vëlla' brother
vërtet' really
vërte'të, e truth
vërte'të, i/e true; real
vështi'rë, i/e difficult; hard
vështirësi' trouble; problem
vëzhgu'es observer
vij come
vit year
Vi'ti i Ri' New Year
vi'zë visa
vizitoj' visit v.
vizitor' visitor
vjedh steal v.
vje'dhje theft
vje'shtë autumn; fall
vje'tër, i/e old; ancient
vle'rë value
vo'gël, i/e small

vo'në late
vo'të voice; vote
votim' voting
voti'me elections
vra'nët, i/e cloudy
vrapoj' run v.; **vrapo!** run!
vra'rë, i/e murdered
vras kill v.
vra'sës killer
vra'sje murder; assassination
vri'më hole

Xh

xhake'të jacket
xheloz' jealous

Y

yll star
y'në our

Z

zako'ne customs (in a culture)
zakonisht' usually
zakon'shëm, i/e (-shme) ordinary; usual
zanat' craft; profession; trade
zarzava'te vegetables
zba'thur barefoot
zbe'të, i pale
ze'mër heart
zemëru'ar, i/e angry

ze'ro zero
zë'në, i/e occupied; busy
zën'kë fight
zgjedh choose
zgje'dhje election
zgju'ar, i/e smart
zi', i black
zi'hem struggle; fight v.
zjarr fire; **zjarr!** fire!
zog bird
zo'në area
zo'një ma'am; madam
zonju'shë miss; young woman
Zot God
zotëri' Sir
zo'ti X Mr. X
zy'rë office

Zh

zha'bë frog
zhdu'ket disappear
zhur'më noise
zhurm'shëm, i/e (-shme) noisy
zhvendo'sur, i displaced person
zhve'shur, i/e naked; bare

ENGLISH - ALBANIAN
ANGLISHT - SHQIP

A

ability aftësi'
about për; rreth
absent, to be mungoj'
absolutely krejtësisht'; patje'tër
academic shkollor'
academic year vit shkollor'
accept pranoj'
accident aksident'
account n. llogari'
accountant llogaritar'
across përtej'
adapter transformator'
add shtoj
address adre'së
administrator administrator'; drejtu'es
advertisement njoftim'; rekla'më
advice këshi'llë
afraid of, to be kam fri'kë nga
afraid, don't be mos ki fri'kë; mos u tremb
after pas
afternoon pasdi'te; mbasdi'te
afternoon, yesterday dje pasdi'te
again prap; përsëri'
against ku'ndër
age mo'shë
agency agjenci'
ago, long dikur'; ko'hë përpa'ra
ago, one month një mu'aj më pa'rë

agreeable i kënd'shëm/e ~'shme
agreement marrëve'shje
agriculture bujqësi'
ahead pa'ra; përpa'ra
aid n. ndih'më
aid v. ndihmoj'
aid worker puno'njës i ndih'mave
AIDS SI'DA
air a'jër
airmail po'stë ajro're
airplane aeroplan'; avion'
airport aeroport'
alcohol alkool'
alike i ngja'shëm/e ~'shme
alive i/e gja'llë
all i/e gji'thë
all right shu'më mi'rë; në rre'gull
all, that's kaq ki'sha!
allergic alergjik'
allergy alergji'
allow v. lejoj'
almost pothu'aj; pothu'ajse
alone ve'tëm
already tashmë'
also gjithashtu'
although megji'thëse; ndo'nëse
always gjithmo'në; gjithnjë'
amazing i mahnit'shëm/e ~'shme
ambulance a'utoambulan'cë
American amerikan', -'ne
among ndërmjet'
amount shu'më
amputation pre'rje gjymty're
anaemia anemi'
ancient i/e la'shtë
and dhe; e'dhe

angry i/e nxe'hur; i/e zemëru'ar
animal ka'fshë
ankle ny'jë e kë'mbës
anniversary përvjetor'
annoy v. nxeh; zemëroj'; inatos'
annoying i bezdis'shëm/e ~'shme
another një tje'tër; e'dhe një
answer n. përgji'gje; v. përgji'gjem
ant mi'zë dhe'u; milingo'në
any case, in sidoqo'ftë
anyhow sidoqo'ftë
anyone kushdo'; cilido'
anything çfarëdoqo'ftë; çdo gjë
anyway sidoqo'ftë
anywhere kudoqo'ftë; kudo'
apart veçan'
apart, to take ndaj veçan'
apartment apartament'
apartment block pallat' bani'mi
appendicitis apendisit'
appetite oreks'
apple mo'llë
appointment takim'
appreciate çmoj
April prill
Arab; Arabic arab'
architect arkitekt'
architecture arkitektu'rë
area zo'në
arm krah
army ushtri'
arrest v. arrestoj'
arrest arrestim'
arrival mbërri'tje
arrive mbërrij'; vij
art gallery galeri' ar'ti

article arti'kull
artificial limb gjymty'rë artificia'le
artist artist'
as si; siç
ashtray ta'vëll duha'ni
ask v. py'es; kërkoj'
asleep në gju'më
aspirin aspiri'në
assassination vra'sje
asthmatic astmatik'
at home në shtëpi'; tek ne'
at last! më në fund'!
at least të pak'tën
at te; tek; në
attack n. sulm; v. sulmoj'
attention vëme'ndje
August gusht
aunt te'ze; ha'llë
autumn vje'shtë
avalanche ortek'
avoid shmang; evitoj'

B

baby fosh'një
bachelor beqar'
back adv. pra'pa; mbra'pa
back n. (body part) shpi'në; kurriz'
back up v. përkrah; pra'psem; n. rezer'vë
backache dhi'mbje shpi'ne
backwards mbrapsht; prap'tas
bad i keq/e ~'qe
bag qe'se; thes; çan'të
baggage bagazh'
bakery fu'rrë bu'ke

balcony ballkon'
ball (toy) top; (dance) ba'llo
bank ban'kë
bar (pub) bar; lokal'
barber berber'
bare i/e zhve'shur
barefoot zba'thur
barn koçek'
barren shterp, -'pë
basement bodrum'
basket shpor'të; kosh
bath ba'një
bathe v. la'hem
bathing suit rro'ba ba'nje
bathroom ba'një
bathtub va'skë
battle luftim'; bete'jë
be v. jam (inf: me qe'në)
beach plazh
beans gro'shë; fasu'le
bear n. ari'
bear v. mbart; (tolerate) duroj'
beard mje'kërr
beat v. (hit) qëlloj'; godas'; (win) mund; fitoj'
beautiful i/e bu'kur
beauty bukuri'
become v. bë'hem
bed shtrat; krevat'
bedroom dho'më gju'mi
bee ble'të
beef mish ka'u/lo'pe
beefsteak biftek'
beer bi'rrë
beet panxhar'; rre'pë
before long së shpej'ti
before pa'ra; përpa'ra

begin v. filloj'
beginning fillim'
behind pra'pa; mbra'pa; nga pas
believe v. besoj'
bell zi'le
below po'shtë
belt brez; rrip
bend v. përkul'; kthe'së; bërryl'
best më i mi'ri; më e mi'ra
bet bast
better më i/e mi'rë; më mi'rë
Bible Bi'bël
bicycle biçikle'të
big i madh/e ~'dhe
bill n. fatu'rë; llogari'
bird zog
birth certificate certifika'të li'ndjeje
birth control kontroll' i li'ndjeve
birth li'ndje
birthday ditëli'ndje; **Happy birthday!** Gëzu'ar
   ditëli'ndjen!
bit, a një çi'kë; një co'pë
bite n. kafsha'të; v. kafshoj'
bitter i/e hi'dhur
black i zi'/e ze'zë
black market treg i zi'
blanket batani'je
bleed v. më rrjedh gjak
blind adj. qorr, -'rre; i/e ver'bër
blizzard stuhi' bo're
block n. postbllok'; v. bllokoj'/zë rru'gën
blond bjond
blood gjak
blow one's nose fryj/shfryj hu'ndët
blow up (explode) v. shpërthen'; pëlcet'
blow v. fryn (erë)

blue i/e kal'tër; bojëqi'elli
board n. (wood) dërra'së
boat var'kë
body trup
bomb n. bo'mbë
bone koc'kë
book li'bër
bookstore librari'; dyqan' li'brash
boot çiz'me
border crossing pi'kë kufita're
border kufi'
boredom mër'zi
born i/e li'ndur
borrow v. marr hu'a/borxh
boss shef
bother v. bezdis'
bottle shi'she
bottom fund
box kuti'
boy dja'lë
boyfriend i da'shur
bracelet byzylyk'
brain tru; mend
brainless pa tru; pa mend
brakes (car) fre'na
brassiere sutien'; gjimbaj'tëse
brave trim, -'me; guximtar', -'re
bread bu'kë
break down v. (car) ngec; ndalon' (maki'na)
break n. pushim'; ndërprer'je; v. thy'ej; prish
breakfast më'ngjes
brick tu'llë
bridge u'rë
bring sjell
broken heart dëshpërim'
brother vëlla'

brown ka'fe; bojëka'fe
brush n. fur'çë; v. fshij me fur'çë
bucket ko'vë
bug çim'kë; insekt'; bru'mbull
build v. ndërtoj'
building ndërte'së
bull dem
bullet plumb
burn n. dje'gie; v. djeg
burnt i/e dje'gur
bus autobus'
bus station stacion' autobu'sash
bus stop stacion'/vendqëndrim' autobu'si
business enterprise fir'më; ndërma'rrje
business person tregtar'; afarist'
business tregti'; biznes'
busy i/e zë'në (me pu'në)
but por
butcher kasap'
butter gjal'pë
butterfly flu'tur
buy blej
by nga; prej
by the way me që ra' fja'la

C

cake kek; ëmbëlsi'rë
calculator kalkulatri'çe
call n. thi'rrje; v. marr (në telefon'); thërras'; qu'aj
camera aparat' (fotografik')
camping kamp; kamping'
can n. konser'vë
can opener ha'pës konser'vash
can v. mund; mu'ndem

cancel v. anulloj'
cancellation anullim'
cancer kan'ser
candle qiri'
candy sheqer'kë; bonbo'ne
cap kaske'të
capital city kry'eqytet'
car vetu'rë; maki'në; automobil'
care about - I don't care about it aq më bën';
    s'çaj ko'kë; s'prish pu'në
care n. kujdes'
care, take (be careful!) kujdes'!; ru'hu!
care, take care of... kujde'sem për...
career karie'rë
careful i kujdes'shëm/e ~'shme
caress përkëdhe'lje
carpenter marangoz'
carpet qilim'
cash n. para'; të ho'lla
castle kështje'llë
casual jozyrtar'; i/e shkujde'sur
casualty vikti'më
cat ma'ce
catch v. kap; **catch a cold** marr të ftoh'të; fto'hem
cattle gje'dhë; bagëti'
cause n. shkak; v. shkaktoj'
cave shpe'llë
cease-fire armëpushim'
cease n. pushim'
cellar bodrum'
cemetery varre'zë
center qe'ndër
century she'kull
certain i/e si'gurt
certainly sigurisht'
chain zinxhir'

chair karri'ge
chance rast; shans; rastësi'
chance, by rastësisht'; për shans
change n. ndryshim'; (of money) kë'mbim;
    parash; (small money) të ho'lla; të vo'gla;
    v. ndërroj' vend
charge përgjegjësi'; dety'rë
charity bamirësi'
charming tërhe'qës, -e; i hirshëm/e ~'shme
chase ndje'kje
cheap (not expensive) i/e li'rë; (low quality) i/e
    do'bët
cheat v. mashtroj'; bëj hi'le
check n. fatu'rë; llogari'; çek; v. kontrolloj'
cheese dja'thë
chess shah
chest gjoks
chewing gum çamçakiz'
chicken pu'lë
child fëmi'jë
children fëmi'jë
choice zgje'dhje
choose v. zgjedh
chop bërxo'llë
Christmas Krishtli'ndje; Pa'shkë e Vo'gël
church ki'shë
cigar pu'ro
cinema kinema'
citizen qytetar'
civil rights të drej'tat e njeri'ut
civil war lu'ftë civi'le
civilian civil'
clean adj. i/e pa'stër
clean v. pastroj'
clock o'rë

close a'fër
close v. mbyll
closed i/e mby'llur
cloud re
cloudy i/e vra'nët; me re'
coal mine minie'rë qymy'ri
coat pall'to
coffee ka'fe
coin mone'dhë
cold i/e ftoh'të
college universitet'; fakultet'
color ngjy'rë
comb kre'hër
come v. vij
comfortable i rehat'shëm/e ~'shme
companion shok; shoqëru'es
company shoqëri'; miq; vizito'rë
complaint anke'së
condom prezervativ'
confess pranoj'; pohoj'
confession pohim'
congratulations! uri'me!
consultant këshilltar'; konsulent'
convenient i përshtat'shëm/e ~'shme
conversation bise'dë
convince bind
convoy karvan'
cook n. kuzhinier', -'re; v. gatu'aj
cookies ëmbëlsi'ra; bisko'ta
cool i/e fre'skët
copy n. ko'pje; v. fotokopjoj'
corn mi'sër
corner qo'she; cep; **on the corner** në qo'she; te
  ce'pi
corruption korrupsion'

cost n. çmim; v. kushton'
cough n. ko'llë; v. kolli'tem
count v. numëroj'
country vend; shtet
countryside fshat; naty'rë
couple çift; **a couple** ca; disa'; nja dy'
cousin kushëri'
cow lo'pë
crab gafo'rre
crackers bisko'ta me kri'pë
cramp n. ngërç
crazy i/e ma'rrë
cream aj'kë
crime krim
criminal kriminel'
crisis kri'zë
crops të ko'rra; prodhi'me
cross n. kryq; v. (the street) kapërcej' (rru'gën)
crossroads kryqëzim'
crowd tur'më
crowded i/e mbu'shur
cruel mizor'
cry v. bërtas'; qaj; **don't cry!** mos qaj!
cry brit'më; qa'rje
cucumber tra'ngull; kastravec'
cup filxhan'; go'të
cupboard raft; dollap'; bufe'
currency mone'dhë; para'
customer ble'rës; klient'
customs (at borders) doga'në; (cultural) zako'ne
cut v. pres
cut off (phone call) v. ndërpres' (bise'dën)
cut off a piece v. pres një co'pë

D

dairy bulmeto're
dairy products bulmet'ra
dam n. di'gë
dance n. va'lle; v. vallëzoj'; kërcej'
dancing vallëzim'; kërcim'
danger rrezik'
dangerous i rrezik'shëm/e ~'shme
dark i/e e'rrët
date of... da'ta e...; **arrival date** mbërri'tjes; **date of birth** li'ndjes; **departure date** largi'mit; i'kjes
daughter bi'jë; vaj'zë
daughter-in-law nu'se
dawn agim'
day di'të
dead end rru'gë pa kry'e
dead i/e vde'kur
deaf shurdh, -e
death vde'kje
debt borxh; hua'
decade deka'dë
December dhjetor'
decide vendos'
deep i/e the'llë
deer dre
defeat n. hu'mbje; disfa'të; v. mund
defend mbroj
delay n. vone'së; shty'rje (afa'ti)
democracy demokraci'
democratic demokratik'
demonstration demonstra'të
dentist dentist'
department store dyqan' i madh; ma'po
departure ni'sje

deprive i heq
desk trye'zë; banak'
dessert ëmbëlsi'rë
destroy shkatërroj'; asgjësoj'
devil djall; dreq
diabetic diabetik', -'ke
diagnosis diagno'zë
diarrhea bark; diarre'
dictator diktator'
dictatorship diktatu'rë
dictionary fjalor'
die v. vdes
diesel na'ftë
diet die'të
different i ndry'shëm/e ~'shme
difficult i/e vështi'rë
dig v. gërmoj'
dinner dar'kë
dining room dho'më ngrë'nieje
direct direkt'; i/e drejtpërdrej'të
direction drejtim'
dirty pis; i/e ndy'rë
disability paaftësi'
disappear v. zhdu'kem
disappointed i/e zhgënjy'er; i/e mërzi'tur
disaster fatkeqësi'; katastro'fë
discussion diskutim'
disease sëmu'ndje
disgusting i/e pështi'rë
displaced person (DP) i zhvendo'sur
dispute n. debat'; konflikt'
distance largësi'
distant i/e lar'gët
district rreth
disturb bezdis'; shqetësoj'
divorced i/e nda'rë

do v. bëj
dog qen
doll ku'kull
donkey gomar'
door de'rë
double bed krevat' dysh
double room dho'më dy'she
doubt v. dyshoj'
dough bru'më
down po'shtë
dozen duzi'në
draw vizatoj'
dream n. ë'ndërr; v. ëndërroj'
dress n. fustan'; ve'shje; v. vi'shem
dressmaker rrobaqe'pës
drink n. pi'je; v. pi
drinkable i pi'shëm
drinking water u'jë i pi'shëm
drive v. ngas
driver shofer'
driver's licence paten'të maki'ne; dëshmi' aftësi'e
drug dro'gë
drugstore farmaci'
drum dau'lle
drunk i/e de'hur; i/e pi'rë
dry adj. i/e tha'të
duck ro'së
duck! u'lu!
during gja'të

E

each çdo; seci'li, -'la
each other një'ri-tje'tri
ear vesh

early he'rët
earth to'kë
earthquake tërmet'
easily leh'të; kollaj'
east li'ndje
Easter Pa'shkë (e Ma'dhe)
easy i/e leh'të
eat v. ha
egg ve'zë
either ... or o'se...o'se
elbow bërryl'
elect adj. i/e zgje'dhur; v. zgjedh
election zgje'dhje; votim'
electricity korent'
elevator ashensor'
else tje'tër; **what else?** çfa'rë tje'tër?
embarrassing shqetësu'es
embassy ambasa'dë
emergency exit dal'je siguri'mi; dal'je në rast
    rrezi'ku
emergency urgjen'cë
empty bosh; i/e zbra'zët
end n. fund
enemy armik'
engine motor'
engineer inxhinier'
English anglez', -'ze; (language) anglisht'
enjoyable i kënd'shëm/e ~'shme
enormous vigan'; te'për i madh
enough mjaft
enter hyj; fu'tem
entrance hyr'je
envelope zarf
epidemic epidemi'
epileptic epileptik'
equipment paji'sje

eraser go'më
escape v. shpëtoj'
escape shpëtim'
ethnic cleansing spastrim' etnik'
Europe Evro'pë
even if e'dhe nëse'; e'dhe sikur'
evening mbrë'mje
eventually më në fund
ever ndonjëhe'rë
every çdo; cilido'
everyone kushdo'; të gji'thë
everything çdo gjë; gjithçka'
everywhere kudo'
exactly! pikërisht!
exam provim'
example she'mbull
excellent i/e shkëlqy'er
except përveç'
exchange money këmbej' para'
exchange shkëmbej'
exciting pre'kës; që të rrëmben'
excluded i/e përjashtu'ar
excuse me më fal
exhausted i rraskapi'tur
exhibition ekspozi'të
exile n. mërgim'; dëbim'; i/e dëbu'ar; i/e mërgu'ar
exit dal'je
expect pres; shpresoj'
expel përzë'; dëboj'
expensive i/e shtrenj'të
experience përvo'jë
experienced me përvo'jë
expert ekspert'; specialist'
explain shpjegoj'
explode shpërthej'
explore eksploroj'; studioj'

express (train) ekspres'
express v. shpreh
extra charge page'së shte'së
extra large te'për i madh
extra shte'së; suplementar'
eye sy
eyesight shikim'

F

face n. fyty're
factory fabri'kë; puni'shte
failure dështim'
faint v. më bi'e të fi'kët
fair (just) i/e drej'të
fall (autumn) vje'shtë
fall down bi'e
false i/e rre'më; falls
family famil'je
fan (electrical) ventilator'
fan (of sports) tifoz'
far i/e lar'gët; larg
farm fer'më
farmer fermer'
farther më larg
fast adj. i/e shpej'të; v. agjëroj'
fat n. yndy'rë; adj. i/e shëndo'shë
father baba'
fault n. gabim'
favorite i/e preferu'ar
fear n. fri'kë
February shkurt
fed up with i/e ve'lur; i/e ngo'pur
feel v. ndi'ej; prek

female adj., n. fe'mër
feminine femëror'
fence gardh
ferry ferribot'; traget'
feud armiqësi'; gjak
fever e'the
few, a ca; disa'; pak
field fu'shë
fifteen pesëmbëdhje'të
fifty pesëdhje'të
fight n. luftim'; nde'shje; gri'ndje; v. luftoj'
fighter luftëtar'
file do'sje
fill plotësoj'
film film
final përfundimtar'
finally më në fund
find v. gjej
finger gisht
finish mbaroj'; përfundoj'
fire zjarr; **fire!** zjarr!
firewood dru zja'rri
first i/e pa'rë
fish n. peshk
fishing peshkim'
five pe'së
fix ndreq; rregulloj'
flag flamur'
flashlight fener' do're
flat adj. i/e rra'fshët
flea plesht
flee v. i'ki me vrap; ua' mbath'
flight fluturim'
flood përmby'tje
floor dysheme'

flour mi'ell
flower lu'le
flu grip
fly n. mi'zë
fly v. fluturoj'
fog mje'gull
folk dancing/music va'lle/muzi'kë popullo're
food supply racion' ushqimor'
food ushqim'
fool budalla'
foot kë'mbë
for për
forbid ndaloj'; nuk lejoj'
forbidden i/e ndalu'ar
foreign(er) i/e hu'aj
forest pyll
forever përgjithmo'në
forget harroj'
forgive fal
fork pirun'
form for'më
fortunately fatmirësisht'
forwards përpa'ra
four-wheel drive fuqi' në të ka'tër rro'tat
fracture thy'erje
fragile i/e bri'shtë; delikat', -'te
free adj. i/e li'rë; (no cost) fa'las
freedom liri'
freeze v. ngrin
French fries pata'te të sku'qura
fresh i/e fre'skët
Friday e prem'te
friend mik; shok
frog zha'bë; bretko'së
from nga

front ba'llë; **in front of** përba'llë
frost ngri'cë
frozen i/e ngri'rë
fruit frut
fruit juice lëng fru'tash
fuel karburant'
full i/e plo'të; plot
full moon hë'në e plo'të
funeral varrim'
funny (strange) i çudit'shëm/e ~'shme; për të
   qe'shur
furniture mobil'je
future n. e ardh'me; adj. i ardh'shëm/e ~'shme

G

gain v. fitoj'
game lo'jë
garden kopsht
gas gaz
gasoline benzi'në
gas station pi'kë karburan'ti
general i përgjith'shëm/e ~'shme
generally në përgjithësi'
germs mikro'be
get marr
get out dal
get up v. ço'hem; ngri'hem; zgjo'hem
gift dhura'të
girl vaj'zë
girlfriend e da'shur
give v. jap
give birth v. lind
glad i/e gëzu'ar

glass (material) xham; qelq; (for drinking) go'të
glasses sy'ze
go shkoj; **let's go!** shkoj'më!; ni'semi!
go away! largo'hu!
go out dal
goat dhi
God Zot
gold ar; flori'
good i/e mi'rë
goodbye mirupa'fshim
goose pa'të
gossip lla'fe; thashethe'me
government qeveri'
grandchild nip/mbe'së
grandchildren ni'pa/mbe'sa
grandfather gjysh
grandmother gjy'she
grapes rrush
grass bar
grateful mirënjo'hës, -'hëse
grave varr
Greek grek, -'ke
Greek (language) greqisht'
green jeshil', -'le; i/e gjel'bër
grenade grana'të
grind blu'aj
ground to'kë
grow rri'tet
guest mysafir'; vizitor'
guide n. udhërrëfy'es
guidebook gi'dë turisti'ke
guilty fajtor', - to're
gun revo'le; pistole'të
guy person'; njeri'

H

habit zakon'
hair flo'kë
hairbrush fur'çë flo'kësh
hairdresser floktar'; berber'
haircut qe'thje
hairdryer tha'rëse flo'kësh
half n. gjy'smë
hammer çekiç'
hand n. do'rë
handbag çan'të grash; kule'të
handicraft pu'në do're; zejtari'
handmade i bë'rë me do'rë
handsome i pa'shëm/e -'shme
handy i volit'shëm/e -'shme; praktik'
hangover turbulli'rë
happen ndodh
happy i/e lum'tur; i/e këna'qur
harbor ske'lë; port
hard i/e for'të; i/e rë'ndë; i/e vështi'rë
harm n. dëm; dëmtim'
harvest n. të ko'rra
hat kape'lë
hate v. urrej'
have kam
have to du'het
hay bar; sa'në
hay fever alergji' nga ba'ri
haystack mullar' ba'ri
he ai
head n. ko'kë
headache dhi'mbje ko'ke
headquarters shtab i përgjith'shëm; qe'ndër
health shëndet'
healthy i shëndet'shëm/e ~'shme

hear v. dëgjoj'
heart attack kri'zë ze'mre
heart ze'mër
heat n. nxehtësi'
heater ngro'hës
heaven paraj'së
heavy i/e rë'ndë
heel the'mbër; (of shoes) ta'kë
height lartësi'
hell ferr
hello! tungjatje'ta!; (on the phone) a'lo!
help n. ndih'më; v. ndihmoj'; **help!** ndih'më!
helpful i dobi'shëm/e ~'shme
her asaj'; atë'; i/e saj; **for her** për të'; **with her** me
    të'; **hers** i sa'ji; e; a'ja; të sa'jët; të sa'jat;
    herself (ajo') ve'të; **that's hers** ë'shtë i sa'ji/e
    sa'ja
herbs bari'shte
here këtu'; **here she comes** ja ku ë'shtë (ajo');
    here you are! (giving sth.) urdhëro'ni!
hide v. fshi'hem
high i/e lar'të
highway rru'gë automobilisti'ke
hike n. e'cje; udhëtim' më kë'mbë
hill ko'dër
him atij'; atë; **for him** për të'; **with him** me të';
    himself (ai') ve'të
his i ti'ji; e ti'ja; të ti'jët; të ti'jat; **that's his** ë'shtë i
    ti'ji/e ti'ja
hit v. godas'
hitchhiking autostop'
hold v. mbaj
hole vri'më
holiday fe'stë; pushim'
home shtëpi'
homemade shtëpi'je

homesick i/e mallu'ar; **I am homesick** më ka
    ma'rrë ma'lli për shtëpi'në
honest i nder'shëm/e ~'shme
honestly? ndershmërisht?
honey mjal'të; **come here, honey** e'ja këtu', shpirt
honor nder
horse and cart karro'cë me ka'lë
horse ka'lë
horse riding sheti'tje me ka'lë
hospital spital'
hospitality mikpri'tje
hostage peng; rob
hostel bujti'në; hotel'
hot food ushqim' i ngroh'të
hot i/e nxeh'të; i ngroh'të
hot water u'jë i ngroh'të
hour o'rë
house shtëpi'
housing project ndërtim' bane'sash
how si
however sidoqo'ftë; megjithatë'
human njerëzor'
human rights të drej'ta të njeri'ut
humid i/e la'gësht
humor humor'; **sense of humor** ndje'një humo'ri;
    humor'
hundred njëqind'
hungry i/e uri'tur
hurry n. nxitim'
hurry up! nxito'!
hurt v. vras; lëndoj'; dhemb; **hurt someone**
    lëndoj' dikë'
husband bu'rrë; bashkëshort'

I

I u'në
ice a'kull
ice cream akullo're
idea ide'; mendim'
identification dokument' personal'; letërnjoftim'
if nëse'; në qo'ftë se
ill i/e sëmu'rë
immediately menjëhe're
immigration imigrim'
importance rëndësi'
important i rëndësi'shëm/e ~'shme
impossible i/e pamu'ndur
improvement përmirësim'
in në
included i/e përfshi'rë
income të ar'dhura
inconvenient i papërshtat'shëm/e ~'shme
incredible i pabesue'shëm/e ~'shme
independence pavarësi'
independent i/e pava'rur
infection infektim'
information informacion'
inhabitant banor'
injury dëmtim'; vrar'je; plago'sje
in-laws nje'rëzit e gru'as/e bu'rrit
innocent (not guilty) i pafaj'shëm/e ~'shme
insane i.e çme'ndur; i/e ma'rrë
insect bite pickim' insek'ti
insect insekt'
inside bre'nda
instead of në vend të
insult n. fy'erje; v. fy'ej
insurance sigurim'
intelligent i/e zgju'ar

interesting interesant', -e
interpret përkthej'
interpreter përkthy'es
intersection kryqëzim'
into bre'nda në
introduce paraqes'
invasion pushtim'
invitation fte'së
invite ftoj
Irish irlandez', -'ze
iron n. he'kur; v. hekuros'
is ë'shtë
island i'shull
isolated i/e veçu'ar; i/e izolu'ar
it ai; ajo
Italian italian', -'ne; (language) italisht'
itching kru'arje
its i/e tij; i/e saj
itself ve'të

J

jack (for car) krik
jacket xhake'të
jail burg
jam n. reçel'
January janar'
Japanese japonez', -'ze; (language) japonisht'
jealous xheloz'
jeans dok xhins; xhin'se; pantallo'na xhins
jewelry stoli'
Jewish çifut', -'te
jogging e'cje
joke shaka'
journalist gazetar'

journey udhëtim'
judge gjyka'tës; gjyqtar'
July korrik'
jump v. kërcej'; hi'dhem
jumpstart nde'zje me bateri' tje'tër
June qershor'
junk vjetërsi'ra
just now sapo'; tani'
just one ve'tëm një
just right pikërisht' kështu'
just ve'tëm
justice drejtësi'

K

keep mbaj
kettle ibrik'
key n. çe'lës
kidding shaka'
kidnap rrëmbej' (person')
kidney ve'shkë
kids fëmi'jë
kill vras
killer vra'sës
kind adj. i/e mi'rë; i/e da'shur
kind n. lloj; **which kind?** çfa'rë llo'ji?
king mbret
kiss v. puth; n. pu'thje
kitchen kuzhi'në
knee gju
knife thi'kë
knitting thu'rje
knot ny'jë
know di
Koran Kuran'

L

ladder shka'llë
ladies' room ba'nja e gra've
lady zo'një
lake liqen'
lamb qingj
lamp lla'mbë
language gju'hë
laptop computer kompju'ter portativ'
large i madh; e ma'dhe
last adj. i/e fu'ndit; **at last!** më në fund'!; adj. i/e
    kalu'ar; v. zgjat; mban; duron'
late vo'në; **too late** te'për vo'në
laugh v. qesh
laundry rro'ba të pala'ra
law ligj; **against the law** ku'ndër li'gjit
lawyer avokat'
lay shtroj
lazy përtac', -'ce; dembel', -'le
lead (metal) plumb
lead v. udhëheq'
leader udhëhe'qës
leaf fle'të; gje'the
leak n. rrje'dhje; pikim'; v. rrjedh; pikon'
leap kërcim'
learn mësoj'
least më i pa'këti; më e pa'këta; **at least** të pak'tën
leather lëku'rë
leave v. lë; v. i'ki; largo'hem
left (direction) i/e maj'të
left v. (past participle) i'ku; u largu'a
leg kë'mbë
lemon limon'
lend hu'aj; jap hu'a
less më pak

let her go! lë're të i'kë!
let me try më lër ta provoj'
let v. lë; lejoj'
let's go! shkoj'më!; ni'semi!
letter le'tër
lettuce salla'të maru'le
level (gradation) nivel'; (flat) i/e rra'fshët
liberation çlirim'
library bibliote'kë
lie down shtri'hem
lie n. rre'në; gënje'shtër
lies shtri'het; gje'ndet
life je'të
lift mbar'tje me maki'në
lift up ngre
light adj. i/e leh'të
light bulb llam'bë elektri'ke
light dri'të
lighter çakmak'
lighting rrufe'
like adv. si; **like this** kështu'
like v. pëlqej; du'a; dëshiroj'; **do you like..?** dëshi-
    ro'ni...?; do'ni të...?; **I would like to...** du'a të..;
    (formal) do të do'ja të...
lip bu'zë
lipstick të kuq bu'zësh
listen dëgjoj'
little i/e vo'gël; **a little** pak
live v. rroj; jetoj'
lively i/e gja'llë
liver mëlçi'
living room dho'më nde'njieje
lobster karkalec' de'ti i madh
local lokal'; i/e ve'ndit
located i/e gje'ndur; që ndo'dhet
lock n. bra'vë

locked i/e ky'çur
lonely i/e vetmu'ar
long ago ko'hë më pa'rë
long-distance call telefona'të interurba'ne
long i/e gja'të
look for kërkoj'
look out! kujdes'!
look v. (appear) du'ket; (see) shoh; shikoj'
loose i/e li'rë; i lëshu'ar
lose humb; humbas'
lot, a shu'më
loud (voice) i/e lar'të (zë)
lousy i/e do'bët; për fa'qe të ze'zë
love n. dashuri'; **fall in love** bi'e në dashuri'; **make
   love** bëj dashuri'; v. du'a; dashuroj'; **I love you**
   u'në të du'a
lovely i/e bu'kur; i kënd'shëm/e ~'shme
low i po'shtëm/e ~'shtme; i/e u'lët
lower v. ul
luck fat; mbarësi'; **good luck!** të shko'ftë mba'rë!;
   just my luck! më e'ci fa'ti!; **pure luck** pu'në
   fa'ti; thjesht fat
luggage baga'zhe
lunch dre'kë
lung mushkëri'
luxury luks

M

ma'am (madam) zo'një
machine maki'në
mad (angry) i/e nxe'hur; i/e inato'sur; (crazy) i/e
   çme'ndur; i/e ma'rrë
Madam zo'një
made i/e bë'rë

mafia ma'fia
magazine revi'stë
mail n. po'stë
mailbox kuti' po'ste
mailman postier'
main kryesor', -'re
majority shumi'cë
make bëj
male n. ma'shkull
man bu'rrë; njeri'
manager drejtor'; përgje'gjës
many shu'më; **too many** te'për
map har'të
March mars
marital status gje'ndje civi'le
market treg; pazar'
marriage marte'së
married i/e martu'ar
marsh moçal'; këne'të
matches shkre'pëse
matter n. çë'shtje; pu'në; **what's the matter?** si
    ë'shtë pu'na?; v. ka rëndësi'; **it doesn't matter**
    s'ka rëndësi'
mattress dyshek'
may I? a mund?; mu'ndem?
May maj
maybe ndo'fta; mba'se; mu'ndet
me mu'a; u'në
meal vakt; ushqim'
mean adj. i keq/e ke'qe; i lig/e li'gë
mean do të tho'të; ka kupti'min; tregon'
meat mish
mechanic mekanik'
medication ilaç'; bar
medium-sized mesatar', -'re
me, too e'dhe u'në; **for me** për mu'a; **it's me** jam

u'në; **with me** me mu'a

meet takoj'; **let's meet again** tako'hemi përsëri';
nice to meet you gëzo'hem që u njo'hëm

meeting takim'; mble'dhje

mend ndreq

mention përmend'; **don't mention it** s'ka përse'

menu meny'

mess rrëmu'jë

message njoftim'; mesazh'; **leave a message** li'ni
një mesazh'

Mexican meksikan', -'ne

midday mesdi'të

middle mes

midnight mesna'të

milk qu'mësht

mill mulli'

mind - **I don't mind** për mu'a s'ka rëndësi'

mind n. me'ndje; **I changed my mind** ndërro'va
me'ndje

mine n. (coal, etc.) minie'rë; (explosive) mi'në

mine poss. pron. i'mi/i'mja; pl. të mi'të/të mi'at;
it's mine ë'shtë i'mi/i'mja

miner minator'

minority paki'cë

mirror pasqy'rë

Miss n. zonju'shë

miss v. më mungon'; kam mall; **I miss you** kam
mall për ty; **something is missing** diçka'
mungon'; më i'kën; **I missed the train** më i'ku
tre'ni

mistake gabim'

misunderstanding keqkuptim'

mix përzi'ej

mixture përzi'erje

modern modern'

moment çast; moment'

Monday e hë'në
money para'
month mu'aj
moon hë'në; **full moon** hë'në e plo'të
moped (motorbike) motoçikle'të
more më shu'më
morning mëngjes'; **in the morning** në mëngjes'
mosquito mushko'një
most (majority) shumi'ca; **most of the time**
    shumi'cën e ko'hës; **I like that one most** ajo'
    më pëlqen' më shu'më nga të gji'tha
mother në'në
motorcycle motor'; motoçikle'të
mountain mal
mountain pass qa'fë ma'li
mouse mi
moustache musta'qe
mouth go'jë
move v. lëviz'; (change one's residence)
    shpërngu'lem; ndërroj' shtëpi'
movie film
movies kinema'
much shu'më
mud bal'të
mule mu'shkë
murder vra'sje
murdered (m, f, pl) i/e/të vra'rë
murderer vra'sës
muscle mu'skul
museum muze'; muzeum'
mushroom këpur'dhë
music muzi'kë
Muslim musliman'
must v. du'het
mustard mustar'dë
my (m, f, m pl, f pl) im/i'me/e mi'/e mi'a

myself ve'të; u'në ve'të
mystery mister'

N

nail (fingernail) thu'a; (carpentry) go'zhdë
naked i/e zhve'shur; lakuriq'
name n. e'mër; **last/family name** mbie'mër
napkin pece'të
narrow adj. i/e ngu'shtë
nasty i keq/e ke'qe
nation komb; po'pull
national kombëtar'
nationality kombësi'
natural i natyr'shëm/e ~'shme
nausea përzi'erje; të pështje'llë
near adj. a'fër
nearly afërsisht'
neat i/e pa'stër; i/e rre'gullt
necessary i nevoj'shëm/e ~'shme
neck qa'fë
necklace gjerdan'
need n. nevo'jë; v. nevoji'tet; ka nevo'jë; **I need
    him** kam nevo'jë për të
needle gjilpë'rë
negotiator negociu'es
neighbor fqinj; komshi'
neighborhood mëha'llë; la'gje
neither as; asnjë'ri
nephew nip
nervous nervoz'
net adj. ne'to
net n. rrje'të
never ku'rrë
new i ri/ e re

New Year Vi'ti i Ri'; **Happy New Year!** Gëzu'ar
　　Vi'tin e Ri!
news laj'me
newspaper gaze'të
next tje'tri, -'tra
next to pra'në; a'fër
nice i/e mi'rë; i/e da'shur
nickname nof'kë
niece mbe'së
night na'të
nightclub klub/lokal' na'te
nightgown këmi'shë na'te
nightmare ë'ndërr e ke'qe
no jo
nobody askush'; asnjeri'
noise zhur'më
noisy i zhurm'shëm/e ~'shme
none asnjë'; asnjë'ri; askush'
nonsense gje'pura; prof'ka
non-smoking area zo'në ku ndalo'het duha'ni
nor do I as u'në; **nor does he/she** as ai'/ajo'
normal normal'
north veri'
nose hu'ndë
not jo; nuk; **not enough** nuk mjafton'
nothing asgjë'; **nothing else** asgjë' tje'tër
November nëntor'
now tani'
nowhere askund'; asgjëku'ndi
nuisance bezdi'
numb i/e mpi'rë
number nu'mër
numerous të shum'të
nurse infermie're
nuts qiq'ra, lajthi', baja'me, fa'ra etj

O

obey bi'ndem
obligation detyrim'
obnoxious i neverit'shëm/e ~'shme; i
  paduru'eshëm/e ~'eshme
observer vëzhgu'es
obvious i/e qar'të; evident'
occasionally he'rë pas he're; me ra'ste
occupation profesion'
ocean oqean'
October tetor'
odd (strange) i çudit'shëm/e ~'shme; (not even)
  tek, -'ke
of i
off i/e fi'kur
offer n. ofer'të; v. ofroj'
office zy'rë
official adj. zyrtar'; n. zyrtar'; nëpu'nës
often shpesh
oil vaj; na'ftë
OK në rre'gull
old fashioned i da'lë mo'de
old i/e vje'tër; **how old are you?** sa vjeç je?;
  ç'mo'shë ke?
old town qyte'ti i vje'tër; lagj'ja e vje'tër
olive oil vaj ulli'ri
olive ulli'
omelette omële'të
on (not off) i/e nde'zur
on në; mbi
once njëhe'rë; dikur'
once upon a time një he'rë e një ko'hë; dikur'
one-way street rru'gë me një kalim'
one-way ticket bile'të ve'tëm vaj'tje
onion qe'pë

only ve'tëm
open adj. i/e ha'pur; v. hap
opening time o'ra e ha'pjes
operation operacion'
opinion mendim'; opinion'
opportunity rast; mundësi'
opposite adj. i/e ku'ndërt
opposite adv. përba'llë
opposition (party) opozi'të
optimistic optimist'
optional jo i detyru'eshëm; fakultativ'
or o'se
orange portokall'; (color) bo'jë portoka'lli
orchard pemi'shtë
order n. rre'gull; **everything is in order** gjithçka'
    në rre'gull; **in order to** për të; me qëllim' që;
    out of order nuk punon'; i/e pri'shur; v.
    porosis'
ordinary i zakon'shëm/e ~'shme
organize organizoj'
original origjinal'
orphan jetim'
Orthodox Ortodoks'
other tje'tër; pl. të tje'rë/-'ra
otherwise ndry'she
ouch! o'u!
ought du'het
our i/e jo'në
out ja'shtë; **get out!** dil ja'shtë!
outdoors përja'shta; në naty'rë
outside ja'shtë; përja'shta
oven fu'rrë
over mbi; si'për; **over here** këtu'; **over there** atje';
    it's over mbaro'i
overweight mbipe'shë

owe i detyro'hem; i kam borxh; **how much do I owe you?** sa të detyro'hem?

own adj. i/e vet; **my own** i'mi; **on my own** në hesa'pin tim; përgji'gjem ve'të

own v. zotëroj'; kam

owner pronar'

oxygen oksigjen'

oyster go'cë de'ti

P

pack v. paketoj'; mbledh plaç'kat

package pa'ko

padlock dry

paid i/e pagu'ar

pain dhi'mbje

painful i dhimb'shëm/e ~'shme

paint n. bo'jë; v. ly'ej; (artistic) pikturoj'

painting ly'erje; (artistic) piktu'rë

pair çift

pajamas pizha'ma, pizha'me

pale i/e zbe'të

panties mba'thje grash

pants pantallo'na; bre'kë; mba'thje

pantyhose ge'ta

paper le'tër; (newspaper) gaze'të; **a piece of paper** një co'pë le'tër

pardon n. fal'je; v. fal; **pardon me?** (I don't understand) më fal, po s'të kupto'va

parents pri'ndër

park n. park; v. parkoj'

parking lot vend parki'mi; parking'

part pje'së

partner (business) ortak; shok; (sweetheart)
   partner'; i/e da'shur
party (feast) fe'stë; (political) parti'
pass by i kaloj' pra'në
pass out më bi'e të fi'kët
passable road rru'gë e kalu'eshme
passenger udhëtar'
passport pasapor'të
past adj. i/e kalu'ar; n. e kalu'ar; (behind) pas; **just
   past the church** sa kalon' ki'shën
pasta makaro'na
pastime argëtim'
path shteg
patient n. i sëmu'rë; pacient'; adj. i/e duru'ar
pay v. pagu'aj
peace pa'që
peach pje'shkë
peanuts kikiri'kë
pear dar'dhë
pearl per'lë
peas bize'le
peasant fshatar'
peculiar i/e veçan'të; i çudit'shëm/e ~'shme
pedestrian këmbësor'
pee shurroj'
pen pal shok letërkëmbi'mi
pen pe'në
pencil laps; kalem'
people po'pull; nje'rëz
pepper (black, white) piper' (i zi, i bar'dhë);
   (vegetable) spec
percent përqind'
perfect i/e përso'sur
perhaps ndo'fta
period (monthly) perio'da
period of time ko'hë

permanent i përher'shëm/e ~'shme
person njeri'; person'
personal personal', -'le
petrol benzi'në
pharmacy farmaci'
phone telefon'
photograph fotografi'
photographer fotograf'
phrase shpreh'je
piano pia'no
picnic piknik'
picture fotografi'
pie byrek'
piece co'pë
pig derr
pigeon pëllumb'
pill ha'pje
pillow jastëk'
pipe tub; (for smoking) llu'llë
pity gjynah'; **it's a pity** gjynah'; ë'shtë për të
      ar'dhur keq
pizza pi'cë
pizzeria piceri'
place vend; **at my/your place** tek u'në/ti; **place of
      birth** vendli'ndje
plain (not fancy) i/e thje'shtë; (flat land) fu'shë
plane aeroplan'
plant n. (botanical) bi'më; (factory) uzi'në
plate pja'të
platform platfor'më
play n. shfaq'je; v. lu'aj
playground shesh lo'jërash
pleasant i kënd'shëm/e ~'shme
please (like) v. pëlqej'; (pray) v. lu'tem; (satisfy) v.
      kënaq'
pleasure kënaqësi'; **with pleasure** me kënaqësi'

plum ku'mbull
plus plus
pocket xhep
point (period) pi'kë; (meaning) kuptim'; **point at**
   tregoj' me gisht
poisonous i/e hel'mët
police polici'
Polish lustroj'
polite i sjell'shëm/e ~'shme
politician politikan'
politics politi'kë
polluted i/e ndo'tur
pond liqen' (i vo'gël)
pony mëz
pool (swimming) pishi'në; (billiards) bilar'do
poor i/e var'fër; (unfortunate) i/e shkre'të; i gjo'rë
pope pa'pë
popular popullor'
pork chop bërxo'llë de'rri
pork mish de'rri
posh shik
possibility mundësi'
possible i mund'shëm/e ~'shme; **as much as**
   possible sa më shu'më; **as soon as possible** sa
   më shpejt
post (mail) po'stë
postcard kartoli'në
poster afi'she; rekla'më
pot kusi'; va'zo
potato pata'te
pottery e'në bal'te
pour derdh
power (electric) korent'; (might) fuqi'; (political)
   pushtet'
powerful i fuqi'shëm/e ~'shme
practice v. praktikoj'

precious i/e çmu'ar
prefer parapëlqej'; preferoj'
preferably më mi'rë; më te'për
preference preferen'cë
pregnant shtatza'në; me ba'rrë
prepare përgatis'
prescription rece'të
present (gift) dhura'të
present n. e sot'me; e ta'shme; **at present** tani';
    sot; **up to the present** deri tani'; v. paraqes'
president president'; kryetar'
pressure presion'
pretty i/e bu'kur
price çmim
pride krenari'
priest prift
printer maki'në shty'pi; prin'ter
priority përparësi'
prison burg
private privat'; personal'
prize çmim; **win the first prize** fitoj' çmi'min e
    pa'rë
probably me sa du'ket; ka të ngja'rë
problem problem'; **no problem** s'ka problem'
profession profesion'
promise n. premtim'; v. premtoj'
pronounce shqiptoj'
property pro'në
prostitute prostitu'të; kur'vë
protect mbroj
protection mbroj'tje
protest n. kundërshtoj'; protestoj'
proud krenar', -'re
prunes ku'mbulla të tha'ta
public adj. publik'
public holiday fe'stë zyrta're

publicity rekla'më
pull tërheq'
punctual i/e përpik'të
pure i/e pa'stër
purple manusha'qe; bo'jë vjoll'cë
purse kule'të; çan'të do're
push shtyj
put vë

Q

quality cilësi'
quantity sasi'
quarter çerek'
queen mbretëre'shë
question py'etje
queue (line) ra'dhë
quick i/e shpej'të
quickly shpejt
quiet i/e qe'të
quit ndërpres'; lë; **quit smoking** lë duha'nin
quite krejt

R

rabbit le'pur
rabies tërbim'
race (ethnicity) ra'cë; (competition) ga'rë
radiator (heater) kalorifer'; (in a car) fto'hës
railway hekuru'dhë
rain shi
ram dash
Ramadan Ramazan'
rape n. përdhunim'

rare (not frequent) i/e rra'llë
rat mi
rather adv. më mi'rë
raw i/e gja'llë; i/e papje'kur
razor brisk
read v. lexoj'
ready ga'ti; i gat'shëm/e ~'shme
real i/e vërte'të; real'
really vërtet'
reason arsy'e
reasonable i arsye'shëm/e ~'shme
receipt fatu'rë
recently së fu'ndi
recipe rece'të gati'mi
recognize njoh
recommend rekomandoj'
record n. dokument'; do'sje; v. regjistroj'
Red Crescent Gjysmëhë'na e Ku'qe
Red Cross Kry'qi i Kuq
red i kuq/e ~'qe
refrigerator frigorifer'
refugee camp kamp refugja'tësh
refugee refugjat'
regime regjim'
region zo'në
relative n. i a'fërm; kushëri'; farefis'
relax qetëso'hem; çlo'dhem
relaxing qetësu'es; çlo'dhës
relief aid ndih'më humanita're
remain mbe'tem
remember kujtoj'
remote i/e lar'gët
rent n. qira'; v. marr/jap me qira'
repair v. ndreq; riparoj'
repeat përsëris'; **Can you repeat that please?**
  mund ta përsëris'ni, ju lu'tem?

replace zëvendësoj'; ndërroj'
reply përgji'gjem
report n. raport'; v. raportoj'
representative n. përfaqësu'es
request n. kërke'së; v. kërkoj'
require kam nevo'jë për
rescue shpëtoj'
reservation rezervim'
reserved i/e rezervu'ar
resident banor'
rest n. (remainder) kusur'; çlo'dhje; pushim'; v.
çlo'dhem; pushoj'
return n. kthim; v. kthe'hem
return ticket bile'të vaj'tje-ar'dhje
reverse n. i/e ku'ndërt; v. përmbys'
revolution revolucion'
rice oriz'
rich i/e pa'sur
ride n. rru'gë; udhëtim' (me maki'në etj); v. ngas
(maki'nën)
ridiculous qesharak', -'ke
rifle pu'shkë
right (not left) i/e djath'të; (not wrong) i/e drej'të
ring n. una'zë; (telephone) zi'le
ripe fruit frut i pje'kur
risky i rrezik'shëm/e ~'shme
river lu'më
road rru'gë
roadblock postbllok'
rob grabis'; plaçkis'
robbery grabi'tje; plaçki'tje
rock gur
roof çati'
room dho'më
rope litar'
rose trëndafil'

rough road rru'gë e pashtru'ar
round rrumbullak', -'ke
route rru'gë; itinerar'
rubbish pleh'ra
rude i pasjell'shëm/e ~'shme
ruined i/e rrënu'ar
ruins rrëno'ja
run out of... më mbaro'het
run vrapoj'; **run!** mba'thua!
Russian rus, -'se; (language) rusisht'
rust ndryshk

S

sad i/e trishtu'ar
safe i/e si'gurt
safety siguri'
sail v. lundroj'
sailor detar'
sale shi'tje
salt kri'pë
salty i/e kri'pur
same i/e njëj'të
sand rë'rë
Saturday e shtu'në
sausage salsi'çe; suxhuk'
say them
scarf shall
school shko'llë
science shken'cë
scientist shkencëtar'
scissors gërshë'rë
sea det
search v. kërkoj'; kontrolloj'
season sti'në

seat nde'njëse; vend
second (time) seko'ndë; adj. i/e dy'të
secret n. e fsheh'të; sekret'
secretary sekretar'
security sigurim'
see shoh
seed fa'rë
seek kërkoj'
seldom rra'llë
sell shes
send dërgoj'
senior citizens të moshu'ar; pensioni'stë
sense n. shqi'së; ndjesi'
sensible i arsye'shëm/e ~'shme
sensitive i ndie'shëm/e ~'shme
separate v. ndaj; veçoj'; **separated** i/e nda'rë; i/e
    veçu'ar
September shtator'
serious serioz'
service shërbim'
session sean'cë
seven shta'të
seventy shtatëdhje'të
several disa'
shadow hi'je
shallow i/e ce'kët
shame turp
shameful i turp'shëm/e ~'shme
share v. ndaj
sharp i/e mpreh'të
she ajo'
sheep de'le
sheet (bed) çarçaf'
sheet fle'të
shell gua'ckë
shine v. shkëlqen'; ndrit

shiny i ndrit'shëm/e ~'shme
ship ani'je
shirt këmi'shë
shock n. (surprise) trondi'tje; (electric) godi'tje nga koren'ti
shoes këpu'cë
shoot shtij; **Don't shoot!** mos shti'ni!
shop n. dyqan'
shore breg
short i/e shkur'tër
show n. shfaq'je; v. tregoj'
shower dush
shut mbyll
shy i turp'shëm/e ~'shme
sick i/e sëmu'rë
sightseeing vizi'të
sign n. she'një; v. nënshkru'aj; firmos'; **stop sign** tabe'lë ndali'mi
signature nënshkrim'; fir'më
silence qetësi'
silver argjend'
similar i ngja'shëm/e ~'shme
simple (easy) i/e leh'të; (not complicated) i/e thje'shtë
since qysh prej; që nga
sincere i/e sinqer'të
sincerely sinqerisht'
sing këndoj'
singer këngëtar'
single (not married) beqar', -'re
single i ve'tëm/e ~'me
sister mo'tër
sit u'lem; rri u'lur
situation gje'ndje; situa'të
size madhësi'
skilful i zo'ti

skin lëku'rë
skirt fund (grash)
sky qi'ell
slanted i/e pje'rrët
sleep n. gju'më; v. fle
sleeping pills ha'pje gju'mi
sleepy i/e përgju'mur
slim i/e ho'llë
slippers panto'fla
slope pjerrësi'; shpat
sloppy i/e la'gësht
slow i/e ngadal'të
small i/e vo'gël
smart i/e zgju'ar
smell e'rë; aro'më
smelly me e'rë të ke'qe
smile n. buzëqe'shje; v. buzëqesh'
smoke n. tym; v. (smoke cigarettes) pi ciga're
smuggler kontrabandist'
snack vakt i leh'të
snake gjar'për
snow bo'rë
so kështu'
so much së te'përmi; te'për shu'më
soap sapun'
socks çora'pe
soft i/e bu'të
soldier ushtar'
some disa'
somehow disi'
someone dikush'
something diçka'
something else diçka' tje'tër
somewhere else diku' tje'tër
son bir; dja'lë
song kë'ngë

soon së shpej'ti
sorry i/e hidhëru'ar; **I'm sorry** më vjen keq; më
    fal
sort n. lloj
soul shpirt
soup su'pë
sour cream aj'kë
sour i/e thar'të
south jug
Spanish spanjoll', -'lle; (language) spanjisht'
speak flas
speaker fo'lës
special i posa'çëm/e ~'çme
speed shpejtësi'
spell (say letter by letter) them ger'më për ger'më
spend shpenzoj'
spice e'rëz
spicy pikant'; me e'rëza
split ndaj
spoiled i/e pri'shur
sponge sfungjer'
spoon lu'gë
spread shpërndaj'
spring (season) pranve'rë; (water source) burim'
spy n. spiun'
stain njo'llë
stamp n. pu'llë po'ste
stand up ngri'hem
star yll
start n. fillim'; v. filloj'
starving i/e uri'tur
station stacion; **police station** rajon' polici'e
statue statu'jë
stay v. rri
steak biftek'
steal vjedh

steel çelik'
stick (staff) shkop
stingy koprac'
stocks aksio'ne
stone gur
stop v. ndaloj'
store n. dyqan'
storm n. stuhi'
stove so'bë
straight i/e drej'të
strange i çudit'shëm/e ~'shme
stranger i panjo'hur
stream përru'a
street rru'gë
strength for'cë
strike n. gre'vë; v. godas'
string spa'ngo
strong i/e for'të
struggle lu'ftë
stuck i/e nge'cur
student (college) student'; (high school) nxë'nës
stupid budalla', -'qe
suburb rrethi'na
subway metro'
successful i sukses'shëm/e ~'shme
such i/e ti'llë
suddenly papri'tur
sugar sheqer'
suggest propozoj'
suggestion propozim'
suitcase vali'xhe
summer ve'rë
sun di'ell
Sunday e di'el
sunglasses sy'ze di'elli
sunny me di'ell

sunrise li'ndje e di'ellit
sunset perëndim' i di'ellit
surgeon kirurg'
surgery operacion'
surprise habi'; befasi'
swamp moçal'; këne'të
swear beto'hem
sweep fshij
sweet i/e ë'mbël
sweetness ëmbëlsi'
swim notoj'
swimming pool pishi'në
Swiss zviceran', -'ne
switch off fik
switch on ndez
swollen i/e ënj'tur
sympathy keqar'dhje
system sistem'

T

table tavoli'në
tablet ha'pje
tail bisht
take care! të pri'ftë e mba'ra!
take marr
talk v. flas
tall i/e gja'të; shtatlar'të
tampons tampo'ne
tank (reservoir) cister'në
tape n. shirit'
tape recorder magnetofon'
taste n. shi'jë; v. provoj'; shijoj'
tasteless pa shi'jë
tasty i shij'shëm/e ~'shme

tax tak'së
taxi taksi'
tea çaj
teach mësoj'; jap mësim'
teacher mësu'es
team ekip'; skua'dër
tear v. gris
tears lot
teaspoon lu'gë ça'ji
telephone telefon'
television televizion'
tell them; tregoj'
temperature temperatu'rë
temple te'mpull
temporary i përkoh'shëm/e ~'shme
ten dhje'të
tenant qiraxhi'
tent ça'dër; te'ndë
terrible i tmerr'shëm/e ~'shme
thank you falemnde'rit
that ai'/ajo'
thaw n. ngroh'je; v. ngroh; shkrij
theater tea'tër
theft vje'dhje
there atje'; aty'
these këta'/këto'
they ata'/ato'
thick i/e tra'shë
thief vje'dhës; hajdut'
thin i/e ho'llë
thing gjë; send
think mendoj'
third i/e tre'të
thirst e'tje
thirsty i/e e'tur; **I'm thirsty** kam e'tje
thirty tridhje'të

this ky/kjo
those këta'/këto'
thousand mi'jë
three tre
throw up vjell
throw; throw away hedh; flak
thumb gisht i madh (i do'rës)
thunder bubulli'më
Thursday e mërku'rë
ticket bile'të
ticket office biletari'
tie n. krava'të
tie up lidh
tight i/e shtrëngu'ar
time ko'hë
tip (in a restaurant) bakshish'
tire go'më (maki'ne)
tired i/e lo'dhur
tissue shami' le'tre
toast bu'kë e the'kur
tobacco duhan'
today sot
toe gisht kë'mbe
together ba'shkë; sëba'shku
toilet nevojto're; ba'një
tomato doma'te
tomb varr
tomorrow ne'sër
tonight son'te
too (excessive) te'për
too gjithashtu'
tool ve'gël
tooth dhëmb; pl. dhë'mbë
toothache dhi'mbje dhë'mbi
toothbrush fur'çë dhë'mbësh
toothpaste pa'stë dhë'mbësh

top ma'jë
torture n. tortu'rë
total i/e plo'të; total'
touch n. prek'je; v. prek
tough i/e for'të; i/e ser'të
tourist turist'
towards drejt
towel peshqir'
tower ku'llë
town qytet'
toy lo'dër
traffic jam bllokim' qarkulli'mi/trafi'ku
traffic light semafor'
traffic qarkullim'; trafik'
train station stacion' tre'ni
train tren
translate përkthej'
translator përkthy'es
trauma trondi'tje; tra'umë
travel n. udhëtim'; v. udhëtoj
traveller udhëtar'
treacherous tradhtar'
tree pe'më
trouble shqetësim'
trousers pantallo'na
truce armëpushim'
truck kamion'
true i/e vërte'të
truth e vërte'të
try provoj'; përpi'qem
Tuesday e mar'të
turkey gjelde'ti
Turkish turk, -'ke; (language) turqisht'
turn n. kthe'së; (my turn) ra'dhë; v. kthe'hem;
    turn left/right kthe'hem maj'tas/djath'tas

twice dy he'rë
twins binja'kë
typewriter maki'në shkri'mi
typical tipik'

U

ugly i/e shëmtu'ar
ulcer ul'çer
umbrella ça'dër
uncle (mother's side)da'jë; (father's side) xhaxha'
uncomfortable i parehat'shëm/e ~'shme
under nën; po'shtë
understand kuptoj'
unemployed i/e papu'në
unfair i/e padrej'të
unfortunately fatkeqësisht'
unfriendly jomiqësor', -'re
unhappy fatkeq'
unhealthy shëndetlig', -'gë
union (trade union) sindika'të; bashkim
United Nations Ko'mbet e Bashku'ara
university universitet'
unless në mos; veç po qe se
until de'ri; derisa'
unusual i pazakon'shëm/e ~'shme
up, upstairs lart
urgent urgjent'
us ne; ne've
use v. përdor'
useful i dobi'shëm/e ~'shme
usual i zakon'shëm/e ~'shme
usually zakonisht'
U-turn kthe'së e plo'të

V

vacancy dho'më e li'rë/e pazë'në
vacant i/e li'rë; i/e pazë'në
vacation pushi'me
vaccinate vaksinoj'
valley lugi'në
valuable i/e çmu'ar; me vle'rë
valuables se'nde me vle'rë
value n. vle'rë
vase va'zo
veal mish vi'çi
vegetables peri'me; zarzava'te
vegetarian vegjetarian'
venereal disease sëmu'ndje veneria'ne
very shu'më
very well shu'më mi'rë
via në'për; nëpërmjet'
view pa'mje
village fshat
vine hardhi'
vinegar u'thull
violence dhu'në
visa vi'zë
visibility shikim'; dukshmëri'
visit n. vizi'të; v. vizitoj'
visitor vizitor'
vital jetik'
voice zë
vomit vjell
vote n. vo'të; v. votoj'

W

wage rro'gë
wage v. (war) bëj (lu'ftë)
waist bel; mes
wait pres
waiter kamerier'
waitress kamerie're
wake up zgjo'hem
walk v. e'ci
wall mur
wallet kule'të
walnut a'rrë
wander v. bredh
want du'a
war crimes kri'me lu'fte
war lu'ftë
warm i/e ngroh'të
warn paralajmëroj'
wash v. laj
waste n. hu'mbje; shpërdorim; mbeturi'na; v. shpërdoroj'
watch n. o'rë; sahat'; v. shikoj'; vë'shtroj'
water n. u'jë
waterfall ujëva're
watermelon shalqi'
way (road) rru'gë; **this way** këndej'; mëny'rë
we ne
weak i/e do'bët
weapon ar'më
wear vesh; mbaj
weather ko'hë; mot
wedding marte'së
Wednesday e mërku're
week ja'vë

weekend fundja've
weigh peshoj'
weight pe'shë
welcome mirëseer'dhe
well adv. mi'rë; n. pus
west perëndim'
wet i/e la'gët
what çfa'rë
wheat gru'rë
wheel rro'të; (steering) timon'
when kur
where ku
which kush; ci'li
white i/e bar'dhë
who kush
whole i/e gji'thë; i/e të'rë
whom kë; m. ci'lin; f. ci'lën; **to whom** kujt;
    m. ci'lit; f. ci'lës
whose i/e të; m. ci'lit; f. ci'lës; pl. ci'lëve
why pse
wide i/e gje'rë
widow e ve'; veju'shë
widower i ve'
wife gru'a
wild (not tamed) i/e e'gër
win fitoj'; **Who won?** kush fitoi?
wind e'rë
window drita're
windy me e'rë
wine ve'rë
winter di'mër
wisdom mençuri'
wise i/e men'çur
wish n. dëshi'rë; v. dëshiroj'; du'a
with me
without pa

wolf ujk
woman gru'a
women gra
wonder çudi'tem; py'es ve'ten
wonderful i mahnit'shëm/e ~'shme
wood dru
wood; woods pyll
wool lesh
work n. pu'në; v. punoj'
world bo'të
worried i/e merako'sur; i/e shqetësu'ar
worry v. shqetëso'hem
worse më i keq/më e ke'qe; më keq
wrap v. mbështjell'
wristwatch o'rë do're
write shkru'aj
wrong i/e gabu'ar

X

X-ray radioskopi'

Y

yard oborr'
year vit
yellow i/e ver'dhë
yes po
yesterday dje
yet e'nde; **not yet** e'nde jo
yogurt kos
you ti (fam); ju (pl); ty (obj); ju (obj pl)
young i ri/e re
your i/e ju'aj

yours ju'aji (m); ju'aja (f); tu'ajt (pl m); tu'ajat
   (pl f)
youth rini'

Z

zero ze'ro
zipper zinxhir' (pantallo'nash etj)
zone zo'në
zoo park zoologjik'

ALBANIAN PHRASEBOOK

1. MEETING AND GREETING

GREETINGS - PËRSHËNDE'TJE

Try both ways for pronouncing the following greetings: by applying the rules and explanations given in the Pronunciation Guide, and by pronouncing the expressions between brackets as if they were English words. Be careful to distinguish between the real apostrophe ´ and the apostrophe ' that has been used throughout this book to mark the stressed syllable.

Hi!	**Tungjatje'ta!**
	(pronounced:
	ToondgaTYEta)
Good morning!	**Mirëmëngjes'!**
	(pronounced:
	MeermuhndgES)
Good afternoon!	**Mirëdi'ta!** (pronounced:
	MeerdEEta)
Good evening!	**Mirëmbrë'ma!**
	(pronounced:
	MeerMBRUHma)

BECOMING ACQUAINTED - NJOH'JA

Welcome!	**Mirëseer'dhët!**
Thank you!	**Falemnde'rit!**
You're welcome!	**S'ka përse'!**

Please	**Ju lu'tem**
How are you?	**Si je'ni?**
I'm fine, and you?	**Shu'më mi'rë, po ju?**
Not bad.	**Jo keq.**
What is your name?	**Si qu'heni?**
My name is..	**Qu'hem...**
What do you do?	**Ç'pu'në bën?**
I'm a...	**U'në jam...**
architect.	**arkitekt'.**
doctor.	**mjek; doktor'.**
economist.	**ekonomist'.**
engineer.	**inxhinier'.**
journalist.	**gazetar'.**
computer programmer.	**programist'.**
lawyer.	**jurist'; avokat'.**
nurse.	**infermie're.**
student (in high school).	**nxë'nës.**
student (in university).	**student'.**
teacher.	**mësu'es.**
Where are you from?	**Nga je'ni?**
I'm from...	**U'në jam nga...**
Albania.	**Shqipëri'a.**
America.	**Ameri'ka.**
Canada.	**Kanada'ja.**
Germany.	**Gjermani'a.**
Greece.	**Greqi'a.**
England.	**Angli'a.**
France.	**Fran'ca.**
Italy.	**Itali'a.**
Spain.	**Spa'nja.**
Where do you come from?	**Prej nga vjen?**
I come from Prishtina.	**Vij nga Prishti'na.**

I was born in...	**Kam li'ndur në...**
What is your nationality?	**Ç'kombësi' ke'ni?**
I am...	**Jam...**
American.	**amerikan'.**
Canadian.	**kanadez'.**
German.	**gjerman'.**
Greek.	**grek.**
English.	**anglez'.**
French.	**francez'.**
Italian.	**italian'.**
Spanish.	**spanjoll'.**
How old are you?	**Ç'mo'shë ke'ni?**
I am 45 years old.	**U'në jam dyzetepe'së vjeç.**
Where do you live?	**Ku jeto'ni?**
Pleased to meet you.	**Gëzo'hem që po tako'hemi.**
I'm with the Red Cross.	**Jam me Kry'qin e kuq.**
I don't speak Albanian.	**U'në nuk flas shqip.**
I only speak a little Albanian.	**Flas pak shqip.**
I want to learn Albanian.	**Du'a të mësoj' shqip.**
How long are you going to stay in Albania?	**Sa ko'hë do të rri'ni në Shqipëri'?**
Do you speak English?	**Flis'ni anglisht'?**
A little.	**Pak'sa.**
So-so.	**Disi'.**
Very well.	**Shu'më mi'rë.**
What language do you know?	**Ç'gju'hë di'ni?**
How do you say this?	**Si thu'het?**
I don't understand.	**Nuk kuptoj'.**

Just a minute.	**Një minu'të.**
I would like you to meet...	**Nji'huni me...**
my husband.	**bu'rrin tim.**
my wife.	**gru'an ti'me.**
my daughter.	**vaj'zën ti'me.**
my son.	**dja'lin tim.**
my girlfriend.	**të da'shurën ti'me.**
my boyfriend.	**të da'shurin tim.**
my friend.	**sho'kun tim.**
my colleague.	**kole'gun tim; sho'kun tim të pu'nës.**
my family.	**famil'jen ti'me.**
Are you married?	**Je'ni i/e martu'ar?**
I am married.	**Jam i/e martu'ar.**
I am divorced.	**Jam i/e nda'rë.**
I am widowed.	**Jam i/e ve.**
I am single.	**Jam beqar',-'re.**
Do you have a boyfriend/a girlfriend?	**Ke'ni ndonjë' të da'shur?**
Do you have children?	**Ke'ni fëmi'jë?**
How many children do you have?	**Sa fëmi'jë ke'ni?**
I have a son and a daughter.	**Kam një dja'lë e një vaj'zë.**
I don't have any children.	**Nuk kam fëmi'jë.**
aunt	(maternal) **te'ze**; (paternal) **ha'llë**
boy	**dja'lë**
brother	**vëlla'**
brothers	**vëlle'zër**
children	**fëmi'jë**
cousin	**kushëri',-'rë**
daughter	**vaj'zë; bi'jë**
father	**ba'bë**

family	**famil'je**
grandfather	**gjysh**
grandmother	**gjy'she**
girl	**vaj'zë**
husband	**bu'rrë; bashkëshort'**
man	**njeri'; bu'rrë**
mother	**në'në**
parents	**pri'ndër**
people	**po'pull; nje'rëz**
sister	**mo'tër**
son	**dja'lë; bir**
twins	**binja'kë**
uncle	(maternal) **da'jë**; (paternal) **xha'jë**
wife	**gru'a; bashkëshor'te**
woman	**gru'a**

DEPARTURE, REGARDS - LARGI'MI, TË FA'LA

Where are you going?	**Ku do të shko'ni?**
I'm afraid I must leave now.	**Më du'het të i'ki tani'.**
It was nice meeting you!	**Gëzo'hem që u njo'hëm!**
See you	
again.	**Mirupa'fshim sërish'.**
later.	**Mirupa'fshim më vo'në.**
soon.	**Mirupa'fshim së shpej'ti.**
tomorrow.	**Mirupa'fshim ne'sër!**
So long!	**Mirupafshim!**
Bye-bye!	**Ngjatje'ta!; Mirupa'fshim!**
Good-bye!	**Mirupa'fshim!; Lamtumi'rë!**

Have a nice day! Good-bye.	**Di'tën e mi'rë!**
Good night!	**Na'tën e mi'rë!**
Have a good trip!	**Rru'gë të mba'rë!**
Good luck!	**Qofsh mi'rë!; Të pri'ftë e mba'ra!**
My regards to everybody!	**Të fa'la të gji'thëve!**
Please, give my best regards to your wife.	**Të fa'la gru'as nga a'na i'me.**

2. BASIC WORDS AND PHRASES

yes—no	**po—jo**
here—there	**këtu'—atje'**
a lot—a little bit	**shu'më—pak**
many	**shu'më**
always—never	**gjithmo'në—ku'rrë**
nothing—everything	**asgjë'—gjithçka'**
everywhere—nowhere	**kudo'—askund'**
almost	**pothu'ajse**
exactly	**pikërisht'**
often—seldom	**shpesh—rra'llë**
No problem.	**S'ka gjë.**
Please!	**Ju lu'tem!**
undoubtedly	**pa dyshim'**
I'm sure.	**Jam i si'gurt.**
Of course!	**Natyrisht'!**
At last!	**Më në fund!**
For sure.	**Me siguri'; E si'gurt.**
Come in!	**Hy'ni!**
Come here.	**Haj'de këtu'.**
Come back!	**Kthe'hu!**
Come with me.	**Haj'de me mu'a.**
That's all!	**Kaq ki'sha!**
I forgot.	**Harro'va.**
I remember.	**Më kujto'het.**
I don't know what to do.	**Nuk di ç'të bëj.**
This reminds me of...	**Kjo më kujton'...**
I'm just kidding!	**Bë'ra shaka'!**
My goodness!	**O zot!**
I swear!	**Ju beto'hem!**
Let's go!	**I'kim!; Shkoj'më!; Ni'semi!**
Go away!	**Largo'hu!**

How many—much?	**Sa?**
What kind?	**Çfa're llo'ji?**
Which one?	**Ci'li?**
What does it mean?	**Ç'do të tho'të kjo?**
What does this word mean?	**Ç'do të tho'të kjo fja'lë?**
I've heard about it.	**Kam dëgju'ar për këtë'.**
Come again!	**Haj'de prap!**
Come back!	**Kthe'hu!**
Come here!	**E'ja/haj'de këtu'!**
Come in!	**Hy'rë!**

CONSENT—REFUSAL - PRANIM'—REFUZIM

OK!; That's right!	**Në rre'gull!**
I agree—I am against it.	**Jam dakord'—Nuk e pranoj'.**
I don't agree with you.	**Nuk jam dakord' me ju.**
I doubt it.	**Kam dyshim'; Dyshoj'.**
You are right— You are wrong.	**Ke'ni të drej'të— E ke'ni gabim'.**
I can—I can't.	**Mu'ndem—Nuk mu'ndem.**
No, I can't.	**Jo, nuk mu'ndem.**
I have no objection.	**S'kam kundërshtim'.**
I am against it.	**Nuk e pranoj'.**
I want—I don't want.	**Du'a—Nuk du'a.**
I don't want to...	**Nuk du'a të...**
It's true.	**Ë'shtë e vërte'të.**
It's impossible.	**Ë'shtë e pamu'ndur.**

No, thanks.	**Jo, falemnde'rit.**
It's impossible.	**Ë'shtë e pamu'ndur.**
It cannot be done.	**Pu'në që s'bë'het.**
Are you certain?	**Je i si'gurt?**
I'm absolutely certain!	**Jam krejt i si'gurt!**
I don't believe you.	**Nuk ju besoj'.**

THANKS - FALËNDERI'ME

Thanks!; Thank you!	**Falemnde'rit!**
Thanks a lot!	**Shu'më falemnde'rit!**
You're welcome.	**S'ka përse'.**
Welcome!	**Mirëseer'dhët!**
With pleasure.	**Me kënaqësi'**
It's very kind of you.	**Je'ni shu'më i sjell'shëm.**
Never mind; Don't mention it!	**S'ka përse'!**
It was a pleasure for me.	**I'shte kënaqësi' për mu'a.**

APOLOGIES - NDJE'SA

Excuse me!; Sorry!	**Më fal'ni!**
I apologize.	**Më fal'.**
I'm so sorry!	**Më vjen shu'më keq!**
I'm sorry for being late!	**Më fal'ni për vone'sën!**
It doesn't matter.	**S'ka gjë; S'prish pu'në.**
It's no bother!	**Nuk më bezdis' aspak'!**
Oh, it's nothing.	**Asgjë' fa're.**
I don't want to bother you.	**Nuk du'a t'ju bezdis'.**

REQUESTS, HELP - KËRKE'SA, NDIH'MË

I need some...	Më du'hen ca...
I'm looking for...	Po kërkoj'...
Will you let me…	A më lejon' të...?
Would you lend me your lighter?	Mund të ma ja'pësh pak çakma'kun?
May I leave this here?	A mund ta lë këtu'?
We need …	Na du'het …
Where is the washroom?	Ku ë'shtë ba'nja?
We would like...	Do të do'nim...
Please bring me...	Ju lu'tem, më sill'ni...
May we look at..?	A mund ta shikoj'më pak..?
Help!	Ndih'më!
Help me, please!	Më ndihmo'ni, ju lu'tem!
I'm lost.	Kam hu'mbur rru'gën.
We are lost.	Ke'mi hu'mbur rru'gën.
I've lost my...	Më ka hu'mbur...
Watch out!	Kujdes'!
May I ask you a question?	Mund t'ju bëj një py'etje?
Will you repeat your question, please?	A mund ta përsëris'ni py'etjen, ju lu'tem?
Where are we?	Ku je'mi këtu'?
Can you help me a little?	Mund të më ndihmo'ni pak?
We want to go to...	Du'am të shkoj'më në...
Where is.... please?	Ku ndo'dhet... ju lu'tem?
Can you lead us to...	A mund të na shoqëro'ni de'ri te...
Do we turn left or right?	Du'het të kthe'hemi maj'tas apo djath'tas?
You are/are not on the right road.	Je'ni/nuk je'ni në rru'gën e du'hur.

Go straight ahead.	**Vazhdo'ni drejt.**
Go this way.	**Kalo'ni kë'ndej.**
May I have a cigarette?	**Mund të më jep'ni një ciga're?**
Yes, please do.	**Po, urdhëro'ni.**
You're welcome.	**Me gji'thë qejf.**
Yes, certainly.	**Sigurisht'.**
By all means.	**Patje'tër.**
With pleasure.	**Me kënaqësi'.**
If you like.	**Po të do'ni.**
As you like.	**Si të do'ni.**
Can you explain that to me?	**Mund të ma shpjego'ni këtë'?**
Please correct me if I make a mistake.	**Ju lu'tem më korrigjo'ni po qe se gaboj'.**
I don't know what to do.	**Nuk di çfa'rë të bëj.**
They have stolen my...	**Më ka'në vje'dhur...**

PLACES - VEND

where?	**ku?**
here	**këtu'**
there	**atje'**
over there	**aty'; atje'**
close; near	**a'fër**
closer	**më a'fër**
far	**larg**
far off	**shu'më larg**
further	**më larg**
How far?	**sa larg?**
left	**maj'tas**
right	**djath'tas**
up	**lart**
down	**po'shtë**

QUANTITY - SASI'

How much/many?	**Sa?**
much; many	**shu'më**
little; few	**pak**
enough	**mjaft**
plenty	**plot**
a great deal of	**shu'më; plot**
too much/many	**te'për**
How large?	**Sa i madh?**

QUALITIES - CILËSI'

angry	**i/e zemëru'ar**
bad	**i keq, e -'qe**
beautiful	**i/e bu'kur**
busy	**i/e zë'në me pu'në**
calm	**i/e qe'të**
cheerful	**i/e qe'shur**
lean	**i/e pa'stër**
clever	**i/e zgju'ar**
disappointed	**i/e mërzi'tur**
dull	**i mërzit'shëm, e -'shme**
excellent	**i/e shkëlqy'er**
excited	**i/e emocionu'ar**
fat	**i/e shëndo'shë**
good	**i/e mi'rë**
good-looking	**simpatik'**
handsome	**i pa'shëm, e -'shme**
happy	**i/e lum'tur**
healthy	**i shëndet'shëm, e -'shme**
heavy	**i/e rë'ndë**
hungry	**i/e uri'tur**
ill	**i/e sëmu'rë**
joyous	**gazmor',-'re**

kind	i/e da'shur
lazy	përtac,-e
lively	i/e shka'thët; i/e gja'llë
mean	i lig, e -'gë
modest	i/e thje'shtë
nice	i kënd'shëm, e -'shme
perfect	i/e përso'sur
polite	i sjell'shëm, e -'shme
proud	krenar',-'re
sad	i/e trishtu'ar
self-conceited	mendjemadh',-'dhe
serious	serioz',-'ze
short	i/e shkur'tër
sincere	i/e çil'tër
strong	i/e for'të
stupid	budalla', -'qe
surprised	i/e habi'tur
tall	i/e gja'të
thin	i/e do'bët
thirsty	i/e e'tur
timid	i/e dru'ajtur
ugly	i/e shëmtu'ar
uneasy	i/e shqetësu'ar
weak	i/e do'bët
worried	i/e merako'sur

3. ACCOMMODATION

I am looking for a hotel.
Kërkoj' hotel'.
Which is the nearest hotel?
Ci'li ë'shtë hote'li më i a'fërt?
Is there anywhere I can stay for the night?
Ka ndonjë' vend për të kalu'ar na'tën?
Where is a good hotel?
Ku ka ndonjë' hotel' të mi'rë?
Where is a cheap/clean hotel?
Ku ka ndonjë' hotel' të li'rë/të pa'stër?
Could you write down the address, please?
A mund të ma shkru'ani adre'sën, ju lu'tem?
I have a reservation.
Kam rezervu'ar dho'më.
There has been a cancellation.
Ë'shtë anullu'ar.
My name is...
Qu'hem...
Do you have any ID?
Ke'ni ndonjë' dokument'?
May I speak to the manager please?
A mund të flas me drejtorin, ju lu'tem?
I would like...   **Du'a një...**
    a single room.   **dho'më te'ke.**
    a double room.   **dho'më dy'she.**
Do you have any rooms for tonight?
Ke'ni dho'ma të li'ra për son'te?
How much is it per night?
Sa kushton na'ta?
It's $50 per day/per person.
50 dolla'rë di'ta për njeri'.
How much is it per week?
Sa kushton për një ja'vë?

How long will you be staying?

Sa ko'hë do të rri'ni?

I'm staying for...   **Do të rri...**

    one day.   **një di'të.**

    a few days.   **disa' di'të.**

    two weeks.   **dy ja'vë.**

I want a room facing the street.

Du'a një dho'më me pa'mje nga rru'ga.

I want a room with a... **Du'a një dho'më me...**

    bathroom.   **ba'një.**

    shower.   **dush.**

    balcony.   **ballkon'.**

Can I see the room?

A mund ta shikoj' dho'mën?

No, I don't like it.   **Jo, s'më pëlqen'.**

Are there any others?   **A ka dho'ma të tje'ra?**

Is there..   **A ka..**

    hot water?   **u'jë të ngroh'të?**

    air conditioning?   **a'jër të kondicionu'ar?**

    a telephone?   **telefon'?**

    laundry service?   **la'rje rro'bash?**

    room service?   **shërbim' në dho'më?**

This room is too...   **Kjo dho'më ë'shtë te'për...**

    big.   **e ma'dhe.**

    small.   **e vo'gël.**

    noisy.   **me zhur'më.**

    dirty.   **e pi'sët.**

    cold.   **e ftoh'të.**

    hot.   **e nxeh'të.**

Does this room suit you?

A ju pëlqen' kjo dho'më?

It's fine, I'll take it.

Shu'më e mi'rë ë'shtë, po e marr.

Is there any place to wash clothes?

Ka se ku të lash rro'ba?

Where is the bathroom?
Ku ë'shtë ba'nja?
Is there hot water all day?
A ka u'jë të ngroh'të gji'thë di'tën?
Can I use the telephone?
A mund ta përdor' telefo'nin?

PROBLEMS - PROBLE'ME

I've lost my key.
Kam hu'mbur çe'lësin.
I can't open/close the windows.
Nuk i hap/mbyll dot drita're ret.
Can I have the key to my room?
Mund të më jep'ni çe'lësin e dho'mës si'me?

There is no	**Nuk ka...**
water.	**u'jë.**
electricity.	**korent'.**

The toilet won't flush.
U'ji nuk shkarkon' mi'rë në ba'një.
The heater doesn't work.
Ngroh'ja nuk punon'.

I need...	**Kam nevo'jë për...**
toilet paper.	**le'tër higjieni'ke.**
soap.	**sapun'.**
clean towels/sheets.	**peshqi'rë/çarça'fë të pa'stër.**
another blanket.	**një batani'je tje'tër.**
a light bulb.	**një llam'bë ndriçi'mi.**
drinking water.	**u'jë të pi'shëm.**

I want a wake up call.
Du'a të më zgjo'ni me telefon'.
Please wake me up at...
Ju lu'tem më zgjo'ni në o'rën...

What is your room number?

Ç'nu'mër ka dho'ma ju'aj?

I'm leaving...	**Do të largo'hem...**
now.	**tani'.**
today.	**sot.**
tonight.	**son'te.**
tomorrow.	**ne'sër.**

I would like to pay the bill.

Du'a të bëj page'sën.

What time must I vacate the room?

Në ç'o'rë du'het ta liroj' dho'mën?

When does the hotel bus leave?

Kur ni'set autobusi i hote'lit?

4. FOOD AND DRINK

ORDERING IN A RESTAURANT

I am hungry.	**Kam uri'.**
I like; I'd like…	**Du'a…; Më pëlqen'…**
I don't like...	**Nuk më pëlqen'...**
Do you like..?	**Dëshiro'ni?**
Do you have..?	**A ke'ni..?**
May I have...?	**A mund të më sill'ni…?**
What is this?	**Çfa'rë ë'shtë kjo?**

What is it made of?
   Me çfa'rë ë'shtë bë'rë?
Does it have meat in it?
   Me mish ë'shtë?
I am a vegetarian.
   U'në jam vegjetarian'.
I would like something without meat.
   Do të do'ja diçka' pa mish.
Sorry, it is not on the menu today.
   Më vjen keq, sot nuk ë'shtë në meny'.
We don't have that item today.
   Sot s'e ke'mi në meny'.
What would you like to eat/drink?
   Çfa'rë do'ni të ha'ni/të pi'ni?
Would you like anything else?
   Do'ni gjë tje'tër?
Would you care for dessert?
   Do'ni ndo'një ëmbëlsi'rë?
We recommend/ we have…
   Ju rekomandoj'më/ke'mi…
Is it spicy?
   Ë'shtë dje'gëse?
I have diabetes.
   U'në jam me diabet'.

Just a little, please.
Pak fa're, ju lu'tem.
A little more, please.
E'dhe ca, ju lu'tem.
That's enough, thanks.
Mjafton', falemnde'rit.
I'm full.
U ngo'pa.
It was delicious, thank you.
I'shte e shij'shme, falemnde'rit.
Anything to drink?
Do'ni ndonjë' pi'je?
I'm thirsty.
Kam e'the.
I'm full.
U ngo'pa.
I've already eaten.
Kam ngrë'në (tashmë').
Bring me a glass of beer/wine, please.
Më sill'ni një go'të bi'rrë/ve'rë, ju lu'tem.
The check, please!
Llogari'në, ju lu'tem!

breakfast	**mëngjes'**
cafe-bar	**bar-bufe'**
dinner	**dar'kë; dre'kë**
eat	**ha**
fork	**pirun'**
knife	**thi'kë**
lunch	**dre'kë**
meal	**vakt**
menu	**meny'**
napkin	**pece'të**
pizzeria	**picari'**
plate	**pja'të**
restaurant	**restorant'**

side dishes	**garnitu'ra**
spoon	**lu'gë**
supper	**dar'kë**
table for three	**trye'zë për tre ve'të**
tablecloth	**mbule'së tavoli'ne**
tablespoon	**lu'gë gje'lle**
teaspoon	**lu'gë ça'ji**
waiter, -tress	**kamarier',-'re**

FOOD - USHQI'ME

biscuits	**bisko'ta**
bread	**bu'kë**
bun	**simi'te**
butter	**gjal'pë; tëly'en**
cheese	**dja'thë**
feta cheese	**dja'thë i bar'dhë**
cornstarch	**niseshte'**
cream	**aj'kë**
dish	**gje'llë**
eggs	**ve'zë**
boiled	**të zi'era**
fried	**të fërgu'ara**
poached	**sy'zë**
scrambled	**të trazu'ara - të fërgu'ara**
whipped	**të rra'hura**
flour	**mi'ell**
French fries	**pata'te të sku'qura**
honey	**mjal'të**
jam	**reçel'**
macaroni	**makaro'na**
margarine	**margari'në**
milk	**qu'mësht**

mustard	**mustar'dë**
oil	**vaj**
olive oil	**vaj ulli'ri**
omelette	**omële'të**
pastry	**pa'stë**
pepper	**piper'**
pickled	**turshi'**
pilaf	**pilaf'**
rice	**oriz'**
roll	**pani'ne**
salad	**salla'të**
cabbage salad	**salla'të me la'kër**
potato salad	**salla'të me pata'te**
tomato salad	**salla'të doma'te**
salt	**kri'pë**
spices	**e'rëza**
soup	**su'pë**
chicken soup	**su'pë pu'le**
fish soup	**su'pë pe'shku**
meat soup	**su'pë me lëng mi'shi**
vegetable soup	**su'pë peri'mesh**
sugar	**sheqer'**
yogurt	**kos**

MAIN COURSES - GJE'LLË

baked food	**ta'vë**
baked lamb and potatoes	**ta'vë qi'ngji me pata'te**
barbecued meatballs	**qo'fte ska're**
dried beans in casserole	**fasu'le jahni'**
meat and white beans	**fasu'le me mish**
broiled lamb and yogurt	**ta'vë ko'si me mish qi'ngji**

macaroni	**makaro'na**
meat and pearl onions	**mish çomlek'**
meat and white beans	**mish me fasu'le**
mutton/pork with vegetables	**mish da'shi/de'rri me peri'me**
oven beefsteak	**biftek' fu'rre**
pie (a flaky pastry)	**byrek'**
cheese pie	**byrek' me dja'thë**
cottage cheese pie	**byrek' me gji'zë**
meat (patty) pie	**byrek' me mish**
spinach pie	**byrek' me spinaq'**
milk pie	**byrek' me qu'mësht**
veal and okra	**mish vi'çi me ba'mje**

DESSERTS & SWEETS - ËMBËLSI'RA DHE KARAME'LE

cake	**kek**
fancy cake	**tor'të**
fruit compote	**kompo'sto**
ice cream	**akullo're**
marmalade	**marmala'të**
pudding	**puding'**
candies	**sheqer'ka**
chocolate	**çokolla'të**

MEAT - MISH

bacon	**proshu'të**
beef	**mish lo'pe/ka'u**
chicken	**mish pu'le**
duck	**mish ro'se**
fish	**peshk**

goose	**mish pa'te**
lamb	**mish qin'gji**
mutton	**mish da'shi**
pork	**mish de'rri**
poultry	**mish shpe'ndi**
rabbit	**mish le'puri**
salami	**sallam'**
sardines	**sarde'le**
sausage	**sallam'**
trout	**tro'ftë**
turkey	**mish gjelde'ti**
veal	**mish vi'çi**

VEGETABLES - PERI'ME

beans	**gro'shë; fasu'le**
cabbage	**la'kër**
carrots	**karro'ta**
cauliflower	**lu'lela'kër**
cucumbers	**tra'nguj**
eggplants	**patëllxha'ne**
garlic	**hu'dhër**
green beans	**gro'shë të njo'ma**
leeks	**presh**
lettuce	**salla'të jeshi'le**
mushrooms	**këpur'dha**
onions	**qe'pë**
parsley	**majdanoz'**
peas	**bize'le**
peppers (green)	**spe'ca**
potatoes	**pata'te**
spinach	**spinaq'**
tomatoes	**doma'te**
zucchini	**ku'nguj të njo'më**

FRUITS - FRU'TA

apples	**mo'llë**
apricots	**kajsi'**
bananas	**bana'ne**
cherries	**qershi'**
figs	**fiq**
grapes	**rrush**
melon	**pje'për**
oranges	**portokaj'**
peaches	**pje'shkë**
pears	**dar'dhë**
plums	**ku'mbulla**
quinces	**ftonj**
strawberries	**luleshtry'dhe**
watermelon	**shalqi'**

DRINKS - PI'JE

bottle of wine	**një shi'she ve'rë**
cup	**go'të**
cup of coffee	**një filxhan' ka'fe**
beer	**bi'rrë**
coffee	**ka'fe**
drink n.	**pi'je**
drink v.	**pi**
juice	**lëng fru'tash**
raki (Albanian grappa)	**raki'**
rum	**rum**
punch	**ponç**
soft drinks	**pi'je fresku'ese**
tea	**çaj**
vodka	**vod'kë**

water	**u'jë**
mineral water	**mineral'**
soda/sparkling water	**mineral' i gazu'ar**
whisky	**ui'ski**
wine	**ve'rë**
glass of beer	**një go'të bi'rrë**

5. GETTING AROUND

Albania, or Shqipëria in Albanian (meaning "the Country of the Eagle"), is predominantly mountainous. It is bounded on the north by Montenegro and Kosova, on the east by the Former Yugoslav Republic of Macedonia, on the southeast and south by Greece, on the west by the Adriatic Sea, and on the southwest by the Ionian Sea. Its mountains cover all its territory except for the coastal lowlands and several river valleys. The Alps of Northern Albania form the southern end of the Dinaric Alps and include numerous peaks higher than 7, 000 feet (2,000 m). The beautiful beaches of Velipojë, Shëngjin, Durrës, Divjakë, Vlorë offer long stretches of golden sand, whereas the Ionian coast at Dhërmi, Himarë, Borsh and Saranda is full of beautiful small beaches just below the mountains of the mainland.

With its 3.5 million habitants living in about 10,600 square miles of its territory, the Republic of Albania is one of the more ethnically homogenous countries in the world: about 98% of its people are Albanians. Another three millions of Albanians live actually outside of Albania's borders, in its neighbouring countries, mainly in Kosova and in the Former Yugoslav Republic of Macedonia. The Albanians are the descendants of the ancient Illyrians, an Indo-European people who inhabited most of the Balkans in ancient times.

About half a million people live in Albania's capital city, Tirana.

DIRECTIONS - Orienti'mi

How do I get to..?	**Si mund të shkoj te..?**
Can you show me where is...	**Mund të më trego'ni ku ë'shtë...**
the bank?	**ban'ka?**
the hotel?	**hote'li?**
the police station?	**rajo'ni i polici'së?**
the market?	**tre'gu?**
the train station?	**stacio'ni i tre'nit?**
the airport?	**aeropor'ti?**
the bus stop?	**stacio'ni i autobu'sit?**
the museum?	**muze'u?**
the university?	**universite'ti?**
How far is the next town?	**Sa larg ë'shtë qyte'ti tje'tër?**
I want to go to...	**Du'a të shkoj në...**
How do I get to..?	**Si mund të shkoj në..?**
Can I walk there?	**A mund të shkoj më kë'mbë?**
Is it near/far?	**Ë'shtë a'fër/larg?**
Are we on the right road for..?	**A je'mi në rru'gën e du'hur për në..?**
It's not far.	**Nuk ë'shtë larg.**
Go straight ahead.	**Vazhdo'ni drejt.**
You're almost there.	**Pothu'ajse ke'ni mbërri'tur.**
It's a couple of blocks down.	**Ë'shtë nja dy bllo'qe më tej.**
Turn left/right...	**Kthe'huni maj'tas/djath'tas...**
at the next corner.	**te ce'pi tje'tër.**
at the traffic lights.	**te semafo'ri.**
three blocks further.	**tre bllo'qe më tu'tje.**
at the crossroads	**te kryqëzi'mi.**
Can I park here?	**A mund të parkoj' këtu'?**

I'm looking for this address.	**Po kërkoj' këtë' adre'së.**
Can you show me on the map?	**A mund të ma trego'ni në har'të?**
How much farther is it?	**E'dhe sa du'am të arrij'më?**
I'm lost.	**Kam hu'mbur rru'gën.**

east	**li'ndje**
west	**perëndim'**
north	**veri'**
south	**jug**
crossroads	**kryqëzim'**
one-way street	**rru'gë me një drejtim'**

SOME PREPOSITIONS - DISA' PARAFJA'LË

about	**rreth; përreth'**
after	**pas**
among	**ndërmjet'; midis'**
at (sb.'s place)	**tek(dikush')**
before	**pa'ra**
behind	**pas**
between	**ndërmjet'**
beyond	**përtej'; mata'në**
except	**përveç'**
for	**për**
from	**nga**
in front of	**përba'llë; përpa'ra**
on	**mbi**
since	**që prej**
through	**përmes'**
to	**tek**

towards	**drejt**
under	**nën; po'shtë**
until	**de'ri (në/te)**
until when?	**deri kur?**
with	**me**
without	**pa**

HITCHHIKING - AUTOSTO'PI

Thank you for stopping.
   Ju falemnde'rit që ndalu'at
Where are you going?
   Ku po shko'ni?
I'm going to...
   U'në shkoj në...
Can you give me a lift to..?
   A mund të më ço'ni de'ri në..?

What is the name of..?	**Si qu'het ky...?**
the lake?	**liqen'?**
the mountain?	**mal?**
the river?	**lu'më?**
the town?	**qytet'?**
How ...	**Sa ...**
deep is it?	**i the'llë ë'shtë?**
high is it?	**i lar'të ë'shtë?**
long is it?	**i gja'të ë'shtë?**
wide is it?	**i gje'rë ë'shtë?**

How many people live there?
   Sa nje'rëz banoj'në aty'?
Thanks for the ride!
   Falemnde'rit për udhëti'min!

Where is ..?	**Ku ë'shtë ...**
the border?	**kufi'ri?**
the checkpoint?	**pi'ka e kontro'llit?**
the roadblock?	**postbllo'ku?**

Is the road passable?

Ë'shtë në rre'gull rru'ga?

Are there any mines nearby?

Ka mi'na në këtë' zo'në?

danger	**rrezik'**
minefield	**zo'në e minu'ar**
Be careful!	**Kujdes'!**
refugee camp	**kamp refugja'tësh**
no entry	**ndalo'het hyr'ja**
emergency exit	**dal'je siguri'mi**

PUBLIC TRANSPORTATION

What public transportation do you have here?

Çfa'rë transpor'ti publik' ke'ni?

Are there traffic lights in the city?

Ka semafo'rë në qytet'?

Can you show me the way to the ...

Mund të më trego'ni ...

| bus station? | **stacio'nin e autobu'sëve?** |
| train station? | **stacio'nin e tre'nit?** |

Where is the ticket office?

Ku ë'shtë biletari'a?

Which bus/train goes to ..?

Ci'li autobus'/tren shkon në ..?

Does it go direct?

A shkon drejt e në vend?

Do I have to change buses/trains?

Du'het të ndërroj' autobus'/tren?

Where do I need to change?

Ku du'het ta ndërroj'?

When does the bus leave for...?

Kur ni'set autobu'si për..?

When is the next bus?
Kur ë'shtë autobu'si tje'tër?
How long does it take to go there?
Sa ko'hë mban de'ri atje'?
What time do we arrive?
Në ç`o'rë mbërrij'më?
Where do you get off?
Ku do të zbris'ni ju?
Could you tell me when to take off?
Mund të më tho'ni kur du'het të zbres?
How long is the rest stop?
Sa ko'hë zgjat ndale'sa?
The bus/train is leaving!
Autobu'si/tre'ni po ni'set!
The bus is packed full.
Autobu'si ë'shtë plot.
Let's wait for the next one.
Pre'sim tje'trin.
Do you go to...?
A shko'ni në...?
Can you pick me up?
A mund të më merr'ni e'dhe mu'a?
I want to go to...
Du'a të shkoj në...
Can you give me a lift?
A mund të më ço'ni me maki' në?
I missed the bus.
Më i'ku autobu'si.

arrival	**mbërri'tje**
bus stop	**vendqëndrim'/stacion' autobu'si**
bus station	**stacion' autobu'sësh**
car	**maki'në/Vetu'rë**
conductor	**fatori'no**

departure	**ni'sje**
driver	**shofer'**
entrance	**hyr'je**
exit	**dal'je**
garage	**garazh'; pi'kë riparim'-furnizi'mi**
get off the bus	**zbres nga autobu'si**
get on the bus	**hi'pi në autobus'**
last stop	**stacio'ni i fu'ndit**
mini-bus	**mikrobus'**
motorcycle	**motoçikle'të**
next stop	**stacio'ni tje'tër**
schedule	**orar'**
taxi	**taksi'**
ticket office	**biletari'**
ticket	**bile'të**
touring car	**mikrobus'**
train station	**stacion' tre'nash**
truck	**kamion'**

6. COMMUNICATIONS

TELEPHONE - TELEFO'NI

I'd like to make a phone call.
   Du'a të bëj një telefon'.
Where is a telephone?
   Ku ë'shtë telefo'ni?
Is there a public telephone nearby?
   Ka ndonjë' telefon' me mone'dhë këtu' a'fër?
May I use the phone?
   Mund ta përdor' telefo'nin?
The phone is out of order.
   Telefo'ni ë'shtë i pri'shur.
I want to call...
   Du'a të marr...
The number is...
   Nu'mri ë'shtë...
What is the area code for..?
   Sa ë'shtë prefik'si për..?
Hello!
   A'lo!
I'd like to speak to...
   A mund të flas me..?
This is...
   Jam...
He/she is not here.
   Ai'/ajo' nuk ë'shtë këtu'.
When will he/she be back?
   Kur mund të kthe'het?
I'll call again.
   Do të telefonoj' prapë.
Don't hang up, please.
   Mos e mbyll'ni telefo'nin, ju lu'tem.

Can I leave a message?
  A mund t`i lë një njoftim'?
Where are you calling from?
  Nga po telefono'ni?
Speak a little louder, please.
  Flis'ni pak më fort, ju lu'tem.
The line is busy.
  Ë'shtë i zë'në.
I've been cut off.
  M`u ndërpre' li'nja.
The lines are down.
  Li'nja nuk punon'.
You are wanted on the phone.
  Ju kërkoj'në në telefon'
Can you hear me?
  Më dëgjon'?
I can't hear you!
  Nuk të dëgjoj'!

IN THE POST OFFICE - NË PO'STË

Is there a mail box nearby?
  Ka ndo'një kuti' po'ste këtu' a'fër?
Where is the post office?
  Ku ë'shtë po'sta?
What time does the post office open/close?
  Kur ha'pet /mby'llet po'sta?
Is there any mail for me?
  Ka ndonjë' le'tër për mu'a?
How long will it take to get there?
  Sa ko'hë do që të arri'jë?
How much does it cost?
  Sa kushton?
It depends on the weight and destination.
  Va'ret nga pe'sha dhe destinacio'ni

How much does a registered letter cost?

Sa kushton' le'tra rekomande'?

I'd like to send an air mail letter/parcel.

Du'a të dërgoj' një le'tër/pa'ko me po'stë ajro're.

This parcel is for London.

Kjo pa'ko ë'shtë për në Lo'ndër.

I'd like some stamps for...

Du'a disa' pu'lla për në...

I want to send a money order.

Du'a të dërgoj para me po'stë.

Can I have a money order form, please?

Më jep'ni, ju lu'tem, një mandatpo'stë?

I want to cash this money order.

Du'a të marr para'të që më ka'në ar'dhur me po'stë.

I want to send an urgent telegram to...

Du'a të dërgoj' një telegram' urgjent' në...

7. SHOPPING

Where is the market?
Ku ë'shtë tre'gu?
I want to go shopping.
Du'a të dal për të ble'rë gjë'ra.
Where can I buy..?
Ku mund të blesh..?
Is there any department store nearby?
Ka ndonjë' ma'po këtu' a'fër?

bakery	**dyqa'n bu'ke**
bank	**ban'kë**
barber	**berber'**
bookstore	**librari'**
clothes store	**dyqan' rro'bash**
department store	**ma'po**
grocery store	**dyqan' ushqi'mesh**
market	**treg; pazar'**
newsstand	**qoshk gaze'tash**
pharmacy	**farmaci'**
shoe store	**dyqan' këpu'cësh**
souvenir shop	**dyqan' kujti'mesh**
travel agency	**agjenci' udhëti'mesh**

Can I help you?
Si mund t'ju ndihmoj'?
I'm just looking.
Du'a ve'tëm të shikoj'.
I'd like to buy...
Du'a të blej...
Where is the footwear counter?
Ku ë'shtë repar'ti i këpu'cëve?
Do you have any..?
A ke'ni..?

Can I look at it?
A mund ta shoh pak?
How much is it?
Sa kushton'?
Do you have   **Ke'ni ndonjë' ...?**
  anything ...
    better?   **më të mi'rë?**
    cheaper?   **më të li'rë?**
    larger?   **më të ma'dhe?**
    smaller?   **më të vo'gël?**
Could you lower the price?
Mund të ma jep'ni më li'rë?
I don't like it.
Nuk më pëlqen'.
I want to return this.
Du'a ta kthej këtë'.
Where is the cashier?
Ku ë'shtë ar'ka?
How much do I have to pay?
Sa du'het të pagu'aj?
That's all I have.
Nuk kam të tje'ra.
There is no more.
Ja'në mbaru'ar.
How much/many do you want?
Sa do'ni?
Would you like anything else?
Do'ni gjë tje'tër?

STATIONARY

ball-pen	**stilolaps'**
book	**li'bër**
clock	**o'rë; sahat'**
magazines	**revi'sta**

map	har'të
paper	le'tër
pencil	laps
postcards	kartoli'na

TOILETRIES - SE'NDE TUALE'TI

aspirin	aspiri'në
baby powder	pu'dër fëmi'jësh
comb	kre'hër
condom	prezervativ'
deodorant	deodorant'
face powder	pu'dër fyty're
face cream	krem fyty're
lipstick	të kuq bu'zësh
nail varnish	manikyr'
perfume	parfum'
shampoo	sham'po
shaving cream	pa'stë rro'je
sunscreen	krem pla'zhi
tissues	shami' le'tre
toilet paper	le'tër higjieni'ke
toilet soap	sapun' tuale'ti
toothbrush	fur'çë dhë'mbësh
toothpaste	pa'stë dhë'mbësh

CLOTHING, FOOTWEAR & SPORTS GOODS - VE'SHJE, KËPU'CË, ARTI'KUJ SPORTI'VË

bag	çan'të
ball	top
bathing trunks	rro'ba ba'nje (bu'rrash)
belt	rrip me'si

bikini	**rro'ba ba'nje (grash)**
boots	**çiz'me**
coat	**pall'to**
dress	**fu'stan**
fishing outfit	**ve'gla peshki'mi**
hat	**kape'lë**
jacket	**xhake'të**
jeans	**xhin'se**
jersey	**fane'llë**
jewelry	**stoli'**
leather gloves	**dore'za lëku're**
pajamas	**pizha'ma**
pants	**pantallo'na**
racket	**rake'të teni'si**
raincoat	**mushama'**
sandals	**sanda'le**
scarf	**shall**
shirt	**këmi'shë**
shoes	**këpu'cë**
skirt	**fund**
slacks	**pantallo'na grash**
slippers	**pando'fla**
sneakers	**këpu'cë atleti'ke**
socks	**çora'pe**
sports shoes	**këpu'cë spor'ti**
suit	**kostum'**
sweater	**tri'ko**
tie	**krava'të**
umbrella	**ça'dër**

ELECTRICAL APPLIANCES - ARTI'KUJ ELEKTRI'KË

adaptor	**transformator'**
light bulb	**llam'bë**

cassette tape	**kase'të magnetofo'ni**
dishwasher	**maki'në la'rëse pja'tash**
dryer	**maki'në tha'rëse rro'bash**
fan	**ventilator'**
flashlight	**elektrik' do're**
hairdryer	**tha'rëse flo'kësh**
iron	**he'kur për hekuro'sje**
radio	**ra'dio**
refrigerator	**frigorifer'**
tape recorder	**magnetofon'**
vacuum cleaner	**fshe'së me korent'**
washing machine	**maki'në la'rëse rro'bash**

PHOTOGRAPHING - FOTOGRAFI

I'd like to have this film developed.
   Du'a ta laj këtë' film.
I'd like my picture taken.
   Du'a të dal në fotografi'.
Can you have our picture taken?
   A mund të na bë'ni një fotografi'?

album	**album'**
battery	**bateri'**
camera	**aparat' fotografik'**
film	**film**
flash	**blic**
photograph	**fotografi'**
snapshot	**ma'rrje në fotografi';** **po'zë**

AT THE GROCERY -
NË DYQA'NIN E USHQI'MEVE

bakery	**dyqan' bu'ke**
confectionary	**bonboneri'**
dairy counter	**repar'ti i bulmet'rave**
dry groceries	**arti'kuj ushqimo'rë**
meat counter	**repar'ti i mi'shit**

8. HEALTH & MEDICAL SERVICES

What's the matter?
    Çfa'rë ke'ni?
I'm not feeling very well today.
    Nuk ndi'hem fort mi'rë sot.
I'm not well.
    Nuk jam mi'rë.
I feel run down.
    Ndi'hem i këpu'tur.
I feel better.
    Ndi'hem më mi'rë.
I'm ill/sick.
    Jam sëmu'rë.
My companion is sick.
    Sho'ku im ë'shtë sëmu'rë.
Take me to a doctor.
    Më ço'ni te mje'ku.
May I see a female doctor?
    Mund të më vizito'jë ndonjë' mje'ke fe'mër?
Please undress.
    Zhvi'shuni, ju lu'tem.
How long have you had this problem?
    Sa ko'hë ke'ni në këtë' gje'ndje?
How long have you been feeling sick?
    Sa ko'hë ke'ni i sëmu'rë?

Where does it hurt?	**Ku ju dhemb?**
It hurts here.	**Më dhemb këtu'.**
I am feverish.	**Kam e'the.**
I can't eat/sleep.	**Nuk ha/fle dot.**
I feel dizzy.	**Kam ma'rrje mendsh.**
I feel better/worse.	**Ndi'hem më mi'rë/më keq.**
I've been vomiting.	**Kam pa'tur të vje'lla.**

I'm...	Jam...
allergic to penicillin.	alergjik' ndaj penicili'nës.
asthmatic.	astmatik'.
diabetic.	diabetik'.
epilectpic.	epileptik'.
pregnant.	shtatza'në.

I have...	Kam...
an allergy.	alergji'.
a bad cold.	ma'rrë të ftoh'të.
chest pain.	dhi'mbje gjok'si.
a cough.	ko'llë.
a fever.	e'the/të nxeh'të.
a fracture.	thy'erje.
a headache.	dhi'mbje ko'ke.
a heart condition.	ze'mër të do'bët.
an infection.	infeksion'.
an itch.	kru'arje.
a running nose.	rru'fë.
a sore throat.	gry'kët.
a sprained ankle.	ndry'dhur ny'ellin e kë'mbës.
a stomachache.	dhi'mbje bar'ku.
a toothache.	dhi'mbje dhë'mbi.
diarrhea.	diare'.
I am constipated.	Jam kaps.

EYESIGHT - SY'TË

I need...	Kam nevo'jë për...
contact lenses.	len'te kontak'ti.
new glasses.	sy'za të re'ja.

I've broken my glasses.
Më ja'në thy'er sy'zat.
Can you repair them?
Mund t`i rregullo'ni?
When can I pick them up?
Kur mund t`i marr?

MEDICATION - BAR'NAT/ILA'ÇET

I need medication for...
Du'a ilaç' për...
How many times a day do I take it?
Sa he'rë në di'të du'het ta pi?
When should I stop?
Sa du'het ta vazhdoj'?
I am on antibiotics.
Marr antibioti'kë.
I have been vaccinated.
Jam vaksinu'ar.
I have not been vaccinated.
Nuk jam vaksinu'ar.
Is it possible for me to travel?
A mund të udhëtoj'?

MEDICAL TERMS - TER'MA MJEKËSO'RË

abscess	**abses'**
acute	**aku'te**
after-effects	**paso'ja**
AIDS	**SIDA**
alcoholism	**alkoli'zëm**
amputation	**pre'rje gjymty're**
anemia	**anemi'**
anesthetic	**anestezi'**

appendicitis	**apendisit'**
asthma	**a'stëm**
blood	**gjak**
blood group/type	**grup gja'ku**
blood pressure	**tension'**
blood transfusion	**transfuzion' gja'ku**
bone	**koc'kë**
bronchitis	**bronkit'**
burn	**dje'gie (nga zja'rri)**
cancer	**kan'ser**
check-up	**kontroll'**
chronic	**kroni'ke**
common	**e rëndom'të**
complaint	**shqetësim'**
complication	**komplikacion'**
consultation	**konsul'të; vizi'të**
contagious/catching	**ngji'tëse**
curable	**e shëru'eshme**
diagnosis	**diagno'zë**
disease	**sëmu'ndje**
epidemic	**epidemi'**
fatal	**vdekjepru'rëse**
flu	**grip**
fracture	**thy'erje**
frostbite	**ngri'rje; morth**
heart attack	**kri'zë ze'mre**
heart disease	**sëmu'ndje ze'mre**
heart failure	**pushim' ze'mre**
hepatitis	**hepatit'**
high blood pressure	**tension ' i lar'të**
hypertension	**tension' i lar'të**
incurable	**e pashëru'eshme**
influenza	**grip**
insomnia	**pagjumësi'**
low blood pressure	**tension' i u'lët**
medication	**bar; ilaç'**

pain	**dhi'mbje**
paralysis	**parali'zë**
personal hygiene	**higjie'në persona'le**
pneumonia	**pneumoni'**
precaution	**ma'sa parandalu'ese**
professional	**profesiona'le**
scald	**dje'gie (nga u'ji)**
serious	**e rë'ndë**
side-effects	**efek'te anëso're**
snake bite	**kafshim' gjar'pri**
sprain	**ndry'dhje**
stomach ulcer	**ul'çer stoma'ku**
surgeon	**kirurg'**
symptoms	**simpto'ma**
tonsilitis	**baja'met**
transfusion	**transfuzion'**
typhoid fever	**ti'fo**

HOSPITAL - SPITA'LI

clinic	**klini'kë**
consulting room	**dho'më vizi'tash**
dermatology ward	**pavijo'ni i dermatologji'së**
emergency room	**pavijo'ni i urgjen'cës**
gynecology ward	**pavijo'ni i gjinekologji'së**
hospital	**spital'**
maternity ward	**shtëpi' li'ndjeje**
neurology ward	**pavijo'ni i neurologji'së**
operating room	**sa'llë operacio'ni**
ophthalmology ward	**okulist**
pediatric ward	**pavijo'ni i fëmi'jëve**
pediatritian	**mjek fëmi'jësh**
pharmacy	**farmaci'**
polyclinic	**poliklini'kë**
surgical ward	**pavijo'ni i kirurgji'së**

waiting room	**sa'llë pri'tjeje**
ward	**pavijon'; repart'**

MEDICATION - ILA'ÇET

antibiotic	**antibiotik'**
antiseptic	**antiseptik'**
aspirin	**aspiri'në**
boric acid	**acid' borik'**
disinfectant	**dezinfektu'es**
drug	**ilaç'**
iodine	**jod**
neomycin	**neomici'në**
ointment	**poma'dë**
painkiller	**qetësu'es**
penicillin	**penicili'në**
pills	**ha'pje**
sedative	**qetësu'es**
sleeping pills	**ha'pje gju'mi**
streptomycin	**streptomici'në**
syrup	**shurup'**
tetracyclin	**tetracikli'në**

PARTS OF THE BODY - PJE'SËT E TRU'PIT

ankle	**ny'jë e kë'mbës**
appendix	**zo'rrë qo'rre**
arm	**krah**
armpit	**sqe'tull**
back	**shpi'në**
backbone	**zhty'llë kurrizo're**
belly	**bark**
bones	**koc'ka; e'shtra**
cheek	**fa'qe**

chest	**gjoks; kraharor'**
chin	**mje'kërr**
ear	**vesh**
eardrum	**timpan' i ve'shit**
elbow	**bërryl'**
eye	**sy**
eyebrow	**ve'tull**
eyelashes	**qerpi'kë**
eyelid	**qepa'llë**
face	**fyty'rë**
finger	**gisht**
fingernail	**thu'a**
fist	**grusht**
foot	**kë'mbë**
forearm	**parakrah'; llë'rë**
forehead	**ba'llë**
gallbladder	**tëmth**
hair	**flo'kë**
hand	**do'rë**
head	**ko'kë**
heart	**ze'mër**
heel	**the'mbër**
intestines	**zo'rrë**
jaw	**no'full**
kidney	**ve'shkë**
knee	**gju**
leg	**kë'mbë**
limbs	**gjymty'rë**
lips	**bu'zë**
liver	**mëlçi'**
lungs	**mushkëri'**
mouth	**go'jë**
nape	**zverk**
neck	**qa'fë**
nose	**hu'ndë**
nostrils	**vri'ma të hu'ndës**

palm	**pëllë'mbë**
pupil	**be'bëz**
rib	**bri'një**
skeleton	**skelet'**
shoulder	**shpa'tull; sup**
shoulder blade	**shpa'tull**
skull	**kaf'kë**
sole	**shpu'të**
spleen	**shpret'kë**
stomach	**stomak'**
teeth	**dhë'mbë**
thigh	**ko'fshë**
throat	**fyt; gry'kë**
thumb	**gisht i madh**
toe	**gisht kë'mbe**
tongue	**gju'hë**
tooth	**dhëmb**
waist	**mes; bel**
windpipe	**gurmaz'**
wrist	**kyç i do'rës**

9. EMERGENCY

Get help quickly!
Kërko'ni ndih'më sa më pa'rë!
Call the doctor/the ambulance!
Thërris'ni mje'kun/ autoambulan'cën!
Call the police!
Njofto'ni polici'në!
This person is injured.
Ky njeri' ë'shtë plago'sur.
This is an emergency!
Ke'mi një rast urgjent'!; Ë'shtë urgjen'te!
There has been an accident.
Ka ndo'dhur një aksident'.
There are people injured.
Ka të plago'sur.
I'll call the police!
Po njoftoj'! polici'në!
I'll get medical help!
Po kërkoj' ndih'më mjekëso're!
Does the phone work?
Punon' telefo'ni?
Where is the nearest telephone?
Ku ka ndonjë' telefon këtu' a'fër?
Is there a doctor near here?
Ka ndonjë' mjek këtu' a'fër?
Could you help me please!
Mund të më ndihmo'ni, ju lu'tem?
Take me to a doctor.
Më ço'ni te mje'ku.
How did it happen?
Si ndo'dhi?
What happened here?
Çfa'rë ndo'dhi këtu'?

Can it be fixed?

A rregullo'het?

Who is in charge?

Kush ë'shtë në dety'rë?

Who's in charge of..?

Kush përgji'gjet për..?

I've been robbed!

Më ka'në plaçki'tur!

My suitcase has been stolen.

Më ka'në vje'dhur vali'xhen.

I've lost my...	**Kam hu'mbur...**
bag.	**çan'tën.**
money.	**para'të.**
passport.	**pasapor'tën.**
wallet.	**kule'tën.**

I want to contact my embassy.

Du'a të li'dhem me ambasa'dën to'në.

I need an interpreter.

Kam nevo'jë për përkthy'es.

DANGEROUS SITUATIONS - SITUA'TA TË RREZIK'SHME

Don't move!	**Mos lëviz'!**
Don't shoot!	**Mos shti'ni!**
Keep quiet!	**Mos u ndi'ej!**
Stop!	**Ndal!**

bomb	**bo'mbë**
bullet	**plumb**
disaster	**fatkeqësi'**
grenade	**grana'të**
gun	**revo'le**
minefield	**fu'shë e minu'ar**

| shell | **pre'dhë** |
| war | **lu'ftë** |

10. TIME

DAYS OF THE WEEK - DI'TËT E JA'VËS

Monday	**E hë'në**
Tuesday	**E mar'të**
Wednesday	**E mërku'rë**
Thursday	**E enj'te**
Friday	**E prem'te**
Saturday	**E shtu'në**
Sunday	**E di'el**

MONTHS - MU'AJT

January	**Janar'**
February	**Shkurt**
March	**Mars**
April	**Prill**
May	**Maj**
June	**Qershor'**
July	**Korrik'**
August	**Gusht**
September	**Shtator'**
October	**Tetor'**
November	**Nëntor'**
December	**Dhjetor'**

SEASONS - STI'NËT

spring	**pranve'rë**
summer	**ve'rë**
autumn/fall	**vje'shtë**
winter	**di'mër**

TIME INTERVALS - PERIU'DHA KO'HE

second	**seko'ndë**
minute	**minu'të**
hour	**o'rë**
day	**di'të**
week	**ja'vë**
month	**mu'aj**
trimester	**tremujor'**
semester	**gjashtëmujor'**
year	**vit**
decade	**dhjetëvjeçar'**
century	**she'kull**
millennium	**mijëvjeçar'**
afternoon	**pasdi'te**
evening	**mbrë'mje**
midday	**mesdi'të**
midnight	**mesna'të**
morning	**mëngjes'**
noon	**mesdi'të**
sunrise	**li'ndje e di'ellit**
sunset	**perëndim' i di'ellit**
now	**tani'**
past	**e kalu'ar**
present	**e ta'shme**
future	**e ardh'me**
today	**sot**
tomorrow	**ne'sër**
yesterday	**dje**
the day after tomorrow	**pasne'sër**
the day before yesterday	**pardje'**

this morning	**sot në mëngjes'**
tonight	**son'te**
last night	**mbrë'më**
yesterday afternoon/ morning	**dje pasdi'te/në mëngjes'**

tomorrow afternoon/
   morning
	**ne'sër pasdi'te/në
	   mëngjes'**

tomorrow night	**ne'sër mbrë'ma**
this week/month/year	**këtë' ja'vë/mu'aj/vit**
last week/month/year	**ja'vën/mu'ajin/vi'tin e kalu'ar**
next week/year	**ja'vën/mu'ajin/vi'tin tje'tër**
always	**gjithmo'në**
never	**ku'rrë**
often	**shpesh**
sometimes	**nganjëhe'rë**
What is today?	**Ç`di'të ë'shtë sot?**
What is the date today?	**Sa ë'shtë da'ta sot?**
What time is it?	**Sa ë'shtë o'ra?**
At what time?	**Kur?; Në ç'o'rë?**
Half past two	**Dy e gjy'smë.**

11. PASTIME

What do you do in your free time?
    Çfa'rë bë'ni në ko'hën e li'rë?
I like to...   **Më pëlqen' të...**
    bike.   **shëtis' me biçikle'të.**
    dance.   **vallëzoj'.**
    fish.   **peshkoj'.**
    go boating.   **shëtis' me var'kë.**
    go out with my   **dal me shoqëri'.**
      friends.
    go shopping.   **dal në'për dyqa'ne.**
    go to concerts.   **shkoj në'për koncer'te.**
    hike.   **shëtis' në kë'mbë.**
    play basketball.   **lu'aj basketboll'.**
    play cards.   **lu'aj me le'tra.**
    play chess.   **lu'aj shah.**
    play pool.   **lu'aj bilar'do.**
    play soccer.   **lu'aj futboll'.**
    play voleyball.   **lu'aj volejboll'.**
    skate.   **bëj patinazh'.**
    ski.   **bëj ski.**
    swim.   **bëj not.**
    travel.   **udhëtoj'.**
    watch TV.   **shoh televizor'.**
    work in the garden.   **punoj' në kopsht.**

What kind of ...   **Çfa'rë ... ju pëlqej'në?**
  do you like?
    animals   **ka'fshësh**
    books   **li'brash**
    cars   **maki'nash**
    clothes   **vesh'jesh**
    drinks   **pi'jesh**
    food   **ushqi'mesh**

movies	**fil'mash**
music	**muzi'ke**
songs	**kë'ngësh**
sports	**spor'tesh**
How deep is it?	**Sa the'llë ë'shtë?**
It's cold/hot today.	**Sot bën ftoh'të/nxeh'të.**
It's cloudy/sunny today.	**Sot ë'shtë ko'hë e vra'nët/me di'ell.**

Have you ever been to..?
Ke'ni qe'në ndonjëhe'rë në..?
Have you ever seen..?
E ke'ni pa'rë ndonjëhe'rë..?
Have you ever heard..?
E ke'ni dëgju'ar ndonjëhe'rë..?
Have you ever tried..?
E keni provu'ar ndonjëhe'rë..?

Would you like to...	**Do'ni të...**
see some photos?	**shiko'ni disa' fotografi'?**
This is...	**Ky/kjo ë'shtë...**
my cat.	**ma'cja i'me.**
my dog.	**qe'ni im.**
my family.	**famil'ja i'me.**
my favorite place.	**ve'ndi im i preferu'ar.**
my friend.	**sho'ku im.**
my home.	**shtëpi'a i'me.**
my home town.	**qyte'ti im.**

Do you have any photos?
Ke'ni ndonjë' fotografi'?
That's nice/beatiful/interesting!
Kjo ë'shtë e kënd'shme/e bu'kur/ interesan'te!
Where/When did you take this photo?
Ku/Kur e ke'ni bë'rë këtë' fotografi'?

I really like them!
   Më pëlqej'në vërtet!

12. FEELINGS & PERSONAL QUALITIES

FEELINGS

How do you feel?	**Si ndi'hesh?**
I feel... (I am)	**Ndi'hem...**
afraid.	**i/e tre'mbur.**
angry.	**i/e zemëru'ar.**
annoyed.	**i/e nxe'hur.**
ashamed.	**i/e turpëru'ar.**
bored.	**i/e mërzi'tur.**
comfortable.	**rehat'.**
confident.	**i/e si'gurt.**
confused.	**i/e çorodi'tur.**
disappointed.	**i/e mërzi'tur; i/e zhgënjy'er.**
disgusted.	**i/e neveri'tur.**
excited.	**i/e eksitu'ar.**
exhausted.	**i/e rraskapi'tur.**
frustrated.	**i/e irritu'ar.**
happy.	**i/e lum'tur; i/e këna'qur.**
homesick.	**i/e mallu'ar.**
hopeful.	**plot shpre'së.**
hopeless.	**i/e pashpre'së.**
hurt.	**i/e lëndu'ar; i/e pre'kur.**
jealous.	**xheloz',-'ze.**
lonely.	**i/e vetmu'ar.**
lousy.	**për ibret'.**
mystified.	**i/e shasti'sur.**
pleased.	**i/e këna'qur.**
proud.	**krenar',-'re.**
sad.	**i/e trishtu'ar.**

shocked.	i/e trondi'tur.
surprised.	i/e habi'tur.
tired.	i/e lo'dhur.
uncomfortable.	në siklet'.
worried.	i/e merako'sur; i/e shqetësu'ar.
I'm happy with it.	Më pëlqen'.

QUALITIES - CILËSI'

assertive	i/e si'gurt në vetve'te
capable	i/e a'ftë
cheerful	i/e gëzu'ar
determined	i/e vendo'sur
enthusiastic	entuziast',-'ste
friendly	miqësor',-'re
honest	i ndershëm, e -'shme
organized	i rre'gullt
patient.	i/e duru'ar
reliable	i/e besu'ar
resourceful	i/e shka'thët; i/e çallti'sur
responsible	i përgjegj'shëm, e -'shme
thorough	i përpik'të

13. NUMBERS

0	ze'ro
1	një
2	dy
3	tre
4	ka'tër
5	pe'së
6	gja'shtë
7	shta'të
8	te'të
9	nën'të
10	dhje'të
11	njëmbëdhje'të
12	dymbëdhje'të
13	trembëdhje'të
14	katërmbëdhje'të
15	pesëmbëdhje'të
16	gjashtëmbëdhje'të
17	shtatëmbëdhje'të
18	tetëmbëdhje'të
19	nëntëmbëdhje'të
20	njëzet'
21	njëzetenjë'
22	njëzetedy'
30	tridhje'të
31	tridhjetenjë'
40	dyzet'
41	dyzetenjë'
50	pesëdhje'të
60	gjashtëdhje'të
70	shtatëdhje'të
80	tetëdhje'të
90	nëntëdhje'të

100	**njëqind'**
101	**njëqindenjë'**
1,000	**njëmi'jë**
1,101	**njëmijenjëqindenjë'**
1,000,000	**një milion'**
1,000,000,000	**një miliard'**

ORDINAL NUMBERS - NU'MRAT RRESHTO'RË

first	**i/e pa'rë**
second	**i/e dy'të**
third	**i/e tre'të**
fourth	**i/e ka'tërt**
fifth	**i/e pe'stë**
sixth	**i/e gja'shtë**
seventh	**i/e shta'të**
eighth	**i/e te'të**
ninth	**i/e nën'të**
tenth	**i/e dhje'të**

OTHER QUANTITIES - MADHËSI' TË TJE'RA

double	**dyfish'**
first of all	**në ra'dhë të pa'rë**
half	**gjys'më**
last	**i/e fu'ndit**
once	**një he'rë**
once more	**e'dhe një he'rë**
quarter	**çerek'**
secondly	**së dy'ti**
single	**i ve'tëm, e -'me; tek,-'ke**

thrice	**tri he'rë**
triple	**trefish'**
twice as much	**dy he'rë më shu'më**
twice	**dy he'rë**

14. CAPITALS, COUNTRIES & CONTINENTS

CONTINENTS

Africa	**Afri'kë**
America	**Ameri'kë**
Asia	**Azi'**
Australia	**Australi'**
Europe	**Evro'pë**

COUNTRIES, NATIONALITIES, LANGUAGES AND CAPITAL CITIES

country	**ve'ndi**
nationality/language	**kombësi'a/gju'ha**
capital	**kryeqyte'ti**
Albania	**Shqipëri'**
Albanian	**Shqipta're/Shqip**
Tirana	**Tira'në**
Australia	**Australi'**
Australian/English	**Australia'ne/Anglisht'**
Canberra	**Kanbe'rra**
Austria	**Austri'**
Austrian/German	**Austria'ke/Gjermanisht'**
Vienna	**Vie'në**
Belgium	**Belgji'kë**

Belgian/French-
  Flemish
	Bel'ge/Frengjisht'
	  Flamande'

Brussels	**Bruksel'**

Bosnia	**Bos'nje**
Bosnian	**Bosnja'ke**
Sarajevo	**Saraje'vë**
Bulgaria	**Bullgari'**
Bulgarian	**Bullga're/Bullgarisht'**
Sofia	**So'fie**
Canada	**Kanada'**
Canadian/English-French	**Kanade'ze**
Ottawa	**Ota'vë**
China	**Ki'në**
Chinese	**Kine'ze**
Beijing	**Pekin'**
Croatia	**Kroaci'**
Croatian	**Kroa'te/Kroatisht'**
Zagreb	**Zagreb'**
Czech Republic	**Republi'ka Çe'ke**
Czech	**Çe'ke/Çekisht**
Prague	**Pra'gë**
Denmark	**Danimar'kë**
Danish	**Dane'ze/Danisht'**
Copenhagen	**Kopenha'gen**
England	**Angli'**
British/English	**Britani'ke/Anglisht'**
London	**Lo'ndër**
Finland	**Finla'ndë**
Finnish	**Finlande'ze/-disht'**
Helsinki	**Helsin'ki**

France	**Fran'cë**
French	**France'ze/Frengjisht'**
Paris	**Paris'**
Greece	**Greqi'**
Greek	**Gre'ke/Greqisht'**
Athens	**Athi'në**
Germany	**Gjermani'**
German	**Gjerma'ne/-nisht'**
Berlin	**Berlin'**
Holland	**Holla'ndë**
Dutch/Flemish	**Hollande'ze/Hollandisht'**
Amsterdam	**Amsterdam'**
Hungary	**Hungari'**
Hungarian	**Hungare'ze/-risht'**
Budapest	**Budapest'**
India	**Indi'**
Indian/Hindu	**India'ne/Hindisht'**
New Delhi	**Nju De'li**
Ireland	**Irla'ndë**
Irish/English	**Irlande'ze/Anglisht'**
Dublin	**Dublin'**
Italy	**Itali'**
Italian	**Italia'ne/Italisht'**
Rome	**Ro'më**
Japan	**Japoni'**
Japanese	**Japone'ze/Japonisht'**
Tokyo	**To'kio**

Macedonia	**Maqedoni'**
Macedonian	**Maqedo'ne/-nisht'**
Skopje	**Shkup**
Norway	**Norvegji'**
Norwegian	**Norvegje'ze/-gjisht'**
Oslo	**Os'lo**
Poland	**Poloni'**
Polish	**Pola'ke/Polonisht'**
Warsaw	**Varsha'vë**
Portugal	**Portugali'**
Portugese	**Portuge'ze/Portugalisht'**
Lisbon	**Lisbo'në**
Romania	**Rumani'**
Romanian	**Rumu'ne/Rumanisht'**
Bucharest	**Bukuresht'**
Russia	**Rusi'**
Russian	**Ru'se/Rusisht'**
Moscow	**Mo'skë**
Serbia	**Serbi'**
Serbian	**Ser'be/Serbisht'**
Belgrade	**Beograd'**
Slovakia	**Sllovaki'**
Slovakian	**Sllova'ke/Sllovakisht'**
Bratislava	**Bratisla'vë**
Slovenia	**Slloveni'**
Slovenian	**Sllove'ne/Sllovenisht'**
Ljubljana	**Ljublia'në**

Spain	**Spa'një**
Spanish	**Spanjo'lle/Spanjisht'**
Madrid	**Madrid'**
Sweden	**Suedi'**
Swedish	**Suede'ze/Suedisht'**
Stockholm	**Stokholm'**
Switzerland	**Svi'cër**
Swiss	**Svicera'ne**
Zurich	**Zyrih'**
Turkey	**Turqi'**
Turkish	**Tur'ke/Turqisht'**
Ankara	**Ankara'**
United States	**Shte'tet e Bashku'ara**
American/English	**Amerika'ne/Anglisht'**
Washington, D.C.	**Uashington'**

Other Hippocrene East European Language Titles...

ENGLISH-ALBANIAN COMPREHENSIVE DICTIONARY
60,000 entries • 938 pages • 6 x 9½
hardcover: ISBN 0-7818-0510-4 • $60.00hc • (615)
paperback • ISBN 0-7818-0792-1 • $35.00 • (305)

ALBANIAN-ENGLISH/ENGLISH-ALBANIAN PRACTICAL DICTIONARY
18,000 entries • 400 pages • 4³/₈ x 7 • ISBN 0-7818- 0419-1 •
$14.95pb • (483)

BEST OF ALBANIAN COOKING: FAVORITE FAMILY RECIPES
168 pages • 5½ x 8½ • ISBN 0-7818-0609-7 • $22.50hc • (721)

BOSNIAN-ENGLISH/ENGLISH-BOSNIAN CONCISE DICTIONARY
8,500 pages • 332 pages • 4 x 6 • ISBN 0-7818-0276-8 •
$14.95pb • (329)

BOSNIAN-ENGLISH/ENGLISH-BOSNIAN DICTIONARY AND PHRASEBOOK
1,500 entries • 171 pages • 3¾ x 7 • ISBN 0-7818-0596-1 •
$11.95pb • (691)

BULGARIAN-ENGLISH/ ENGLISH-BULGARIAN PRACTICAL DICTIONARY
6,500 entries • 323 pages • 4³/₈ x 7 • ISBN 0-87052-145-4 •
$14.95pb • (331)

BEGINNER'S BULGARIAN
207 pages • 5½ x 8½ • ISBN 0-7818-0300-4 • $9.95pb • (76)

BYELORUSSIAN-ENGLISH/ENGLISH-BYELORUSSIAN CONCISE DICTIONARY
6,500 entries • 290 pages • 4 x 6 • ISBN 0-87052-114-4 •
$9.95pb • (395)

CROATIAN-ENGLISH/ ENGLISH-CROATIAN
DICTIONARY AND PHRASEBOOK
1,800 entries • 272 pages • 3¾ x 7 • ISBN 0-7818-0810-3 •
$11.95pb • (111)

CZECH-ENGLISH/ENGLISH-CZECH
STANDARD DICTIONARY
10TH Revised Edition
40,000 entries • 1,072 pages • 4½ x 7 • ISBN 0-7818-0653-4 •
$39.50hc • (740)

CZECH-ENGLISH/ENGLISH-CZECH
CONCISE DICTIONARY
7,500 entries • 594 pages • 4 x 6 • ISBN 0-87052-981-1 •
$11.95pb • (276)

CZECH HANDY EXTRA DICTIONARY
2,600 entries • 186 pages • 5 x 7 • ISBN 0-7818-0138-9 •
$8.95pb • (63)

HUNGARIAN-ENGLISH/ENGLISH-
HUNGARIAN CONCISE DICTIONARY
7,000 entries · 200 pages · 5 ½ x 7
ISBN 0-7818-0317-9 · $14.95pb · (40)

LATVIAN-ENGLISH/ENGLISH-LATVIAN
PRACTICAL DICTIONARY
16,000 entries • 474 pages • 4³/₈ x 7 • ISBN 0-7818-0059-5 •
$16.95pb • (194)
BEGINNER'S LITHUANIAN
471 pages • 6 x 9 • ISBN 0-7818-0678-X • $19.95pb • (764)

LITHUANIAN-ENGLISH/ENGLISH-
LITHUANIAN CONCISE DICTIONARY
10,000 entries • 382 pages • 6 x 9 • ISBN 0-7818-0151-6 •
$14.95pb • (489)

MACEDONIAN-ENGLISH/ENGLISH-
MACEDONIAN CONCISE DICTIONARY
14,000 entries • 400 pages • 4 x 6 • ISBN 0-7818-0516-3 •
$14.95pb • (619)

ROMANIAN-ENGLISH/ENGLISH-ROMANIAN STANDARD DICTIONARY
18,000 entries • 567 pages • 4½ x 7 • ISBN 0-7818-0444-2 • $17.95pb • (99)

BEGINNER'S ROMANIAN
200 pages • 5½ x 8½ • ISBN 0-7818-0208-3 • $7.95pb • (79)

ROMANIAN CONVERSATION GUIDE
200 pages • 5½ x 8½ • ISBN 0-87052-803-3 • $9.95pb • (153)

ROMANIAN GRAMMAR
100 pages • 5½ x 8½ • ISBN 0-87052-892-0 • $8.95pb • (232)

SERBIAN-ENGLISH/ENGLISH-SERBIAN CONCISE DICTIONARY
14,000 entries • 400 pages • 4 x 6 • ISBN 0-7818-0556-2 • $14.95pb • (326)

SERBO-CROATIAN—ENGLISH/ ENGLISH—SERBO-CROATIAN PRACTICAL DICTIONARY
24,000 entries • 527 pages • 4½ x 7 • ISBN 0-7818-0445-0 • $16.95pb • (130)

SLOVAK-ENGLISH/ENGLISH-SLOVAK CONCISE DICTIONARY
7,500 entries · 360 pages • 4 x 6 • ISBN 0-87052-115-2 • $11.95pb • (390)

SLOVAK HANDY EXTRA DICTIONARY
3,000 entries • 200 pages • 5 x 7¾ • ISBN 0-7818-0101-X • $12.95pb • (359)

SLOVAK-ENGLISH/ENGLISH-SLOVAK DICTIONARY AND PHRASEBOOK
1,300 entries • 180 pages • 3¾ x 7 • ISBN 0-7818-0663-1 • $13.95pb • (754)

SLOVENE-ENGLISH/ENGLISH-SLOVENE MODERN DICTIONARY
36,000 entries • 935 pages • 5½ x 3½ • ISBN 0-7818-0252-0 • $24.95pb • (19)

UKRAINIAN-ENGLISH/ENGLISH-UKRAINIAN PRACTICAL DICTIONARY
Revised Edition with Menu Terms
16,000 entries • 406 pages • 4½ x 7 • ISBN 0-7818-0306-3 • $14.95pb • (343)

All prices subject to change without prior notice. To purchase **Hippocrene Books** contact your local bookstore, call (718) 454-2366, visit www.hippocrenebooks.com, or write to: Hippocrene Books, 171 Madison Avenue, New York, NY 10016. Please enclose check or money order, adding $5.00 shipping (UPS) for the first book and $.50 for each additional book.